Beginners' UPHOLSTERY TECHNIQUES

Beginners' UPHOLSTERY TECHNIQUES

GUILD OF MASTER CRAFTSMAN PUBLICATIONS

David James

First published 2009
by Guild of Master Craftsman Publications Ltd,
Castle Place, 166 High Street, Lewes, East Sussex BN7 1XU

This title has been created using material previously published in the following
titles: *Upholstery A Complete Course* (first published 1990) and
Upholstery A Beginners' Guide (first published 2004)

© David James 2009

All line drawings by David James

© In the Work Guild of Master Craftsman Publications Ltd, 2009

ISBN 978-1-86108-495-8

Associate Publisher: **Jonathan Bailey**
Production Manager: **Jim Bulley**
Managing Editor: **Gerrie Purcell**
Senior Project Editor: **Dominique Page**
Managing Art Editor: **Gilda Pacitti**
Designer: **Tonwen Jones**

Colour origination by GMC Reprographics
Printed and bound by Kyodo Nation Printing, Thailand

CONTENTS

INTRODUCTION

1

2

3

4

5

6

7

Upholstery is a furniture-making craft, but by nature it also includes elements of soft furnishing, woodworking and occasionally some metalwork. The upholsterer's principal occupation is to furnish and decorate using a variety of materials and fabrics, and therefore a wide range of skills is required. A chair, for example, can contain a huge range of different materials, from shaped metal to the finest silk, and from modern cellular plastics to fine animal hair, such as cashmere.

The type of work can also be quite varied. An upholsterer may be called upon to cover the walls of a whole room with textiles. Folding screens, stools and ottomans are regular candidates for refurbishment, as is bringing back to life an old armchair or sofa.

A chair frame, which is the starting point for most upholstered seating, may be built from formed ironwork, moulded plastics or strong hardwood timbers. The basis of a piece of upholstered seating is the support or the skeleton, usually referred to as the frame, onto which the upholstery is built and fixed.

There are, however, some notable exceptions, such as the beanbag, the floor cushion and the pouffe. All these are self-supporting and have little or no

conventional inner framework. The diverse range of subject matter is all in a day's work for those who take up upholstery. The work is varied, interesting and very creative.

This book aims to guide you through the basics and introduce you to the possibilities. As your skills develop and you become confident with the tools and materials involved, you will begin to create a style and a method of working that you are comfortable with and can enjoy.

Whether you are learning the craft or simply having a go at some basic refurbishment in the home, a knowledge of the structure of a stool, a chair or a sofa will help you to understand the materials used and how they will react to the upholstery process. The beginner can then judge and compare the problems, and also see the possibilities and very often the limitations of a structure.

Furniture construction is a fairly technical business and needs to be precise. Upholstery construction follows a similar pattern, but at the same time will allow you to be creative.

The pleasure of building something with your hands, then adding a dash of colour with your choice of covering, is very satisfying. Equally, trimming and

finishing a piece of work with braid, cording, tassels and buttons is time-consuming and needs care, but an enormous amount of satisfaction can be gained from completing a piece of work.

It is important to work with sincerity and a sense of curiosity, then gradually find for yourself the way you wish to progress. This may be in modern upholstery, traditional upholstery, pure restoration or perhaps a happy combination of all these areas.

It is essential that you base your experience on reliable practices. As your interest grows, your enjoyment will increase, and you will want to share that interest with others. Find out about the work of other upholsterers and compare their methods and techniques with your own progress.

It is fortunate that the upholstery fixed to any framework can be dismantled, usually in the reverse order that it was assembled in the first place. Assuming that it was done well originally, then, with care, tacks and staples can be lifted and the layers of upholstery removed. Although it is not necessary to copy exactly the upholstery that you find, this will be a good starting point. It will provide a useful background for your reupholstery and a point from which the new work can begin.

1 Edwardian Hepplewhite-style mahogany settee

2 Set of Edwardian dining chairs

3 Coronation stool

4 Turned and ebonized French folding stool

5 Original mid-Victorian ottoman with hinged lid

6 Typical 1960s chair

7 Handmade wool tapestry

8 Detailing on a mid-Victorian gilded nursing chair

8

1. TOOLS

The upholsterer's tools range from the most simple and familiar, such as hammers, chisels, scissors and needles, to highly specialized and super-efficient pneumatic and electrical equipment, including staple guns, glue guns, cloth cutters and foam cutters. As a beginner, you should only require the hand tools discussed here.

1.0 Hammers

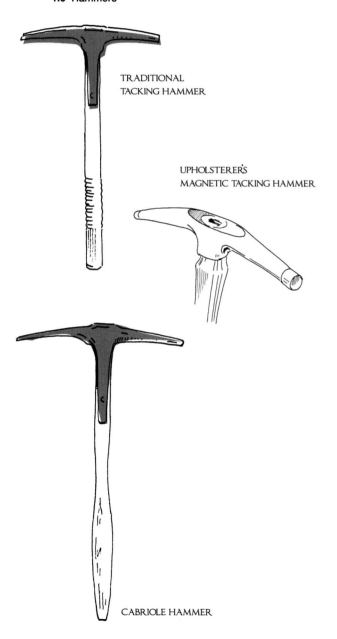

TRADITIONAL
TACKING HAMMER

UPHOLSTERER'S
MAGNETIC TACKING HAMMER

CABRIOLE HAMMER

HAND TOOLS

The hand tools used by the upholsterer are very simple but rather special to the trade. Many are lightweight versions of the cabinetmaker's tools, while others are similar to those used by the carpet layer and by the soft furnisher. Over the past century many of them have been developed and improved, but in general appearance they remain basically the same.

The **tacking hammer** has been the subject of change in that its weight has been increased and the head now has two faces. There are generally three types still available, but the **magnetic hammer with two faces** is without doubt the most commonly used today. The other two versions are a little lighter and more traditional in their design. A **standard tacking hammer** has a single face, a claw and a smooth, round handle. Probably the oldest design of these three is the **cabriole hammer**, which is also used by cabinetmakers. It has a fine small face about ¼in (7mm) in diameter, and a long pear-shaped handle. A small **single-face magnetic hammer** may also be found useful. The various types are illustrated on the left (see 1.0).

It is not necessary to have all three designs of hammer, but every craftsman tends to make a collection of tools over a period of time. An old hammer is seldom thrown away, and new handles made from hickory or ash can easily be fitted to a favourite head.

Upholstery **scissors** or **shears**, of which there are several types, must be of high quality and the very best that can be afforded (see 1.1). It certainly

pays to look around carefully at all the makes and types available, and to try them before buying. As the busy upholsterer will be trimming and cutting all kinds of material for a very large percentage of the workshop time, it is essential that the scissors are always in good condition and kept sharp.

For upholstery work a minimum length of 8in (200mm) for **trimming scissors** is usual. The traditional design is flat and straight, with a blunt end filed smooth and used for tucking away fabric into corners and between chair rails. If maintained and kept sharp, a pair of these scissors will last many years. The **cast-bent shear** has proved more popular, almost certainly due to the fact that its comfortable shape and long blade make it easier to work with and handle for long periods. These shears have a large and a small hand grip, which have angled edges fitting snugly over the fingers and the base of the thumb. Shear lengths range from 8in (200mm) up to 14in (355mm). A pair of 12in (305mm) **cutting shears** is ideal for cover cutting at the table and may also be used comfortably at the bench.

Modern synthetic fabrics can be extremely tough and do demand a keen edge to the blades. The blade tips particularly must be kept sharp, so that the cutting stroke is the full length of the blade, and trimming away excess after tacking is quick and easy.

Regrinding should usually be left to an expert, but maintaining an edge to the blades can be done with care, using a fine flat file or stone. Care should be taken to keep the angle of the cutting edge intact. A spot of oil occasionally at the bolt and a smear of oil along the blades are the only lubrication needed.

A good pair of **8in (200mm) or 10in (255mm) scissors** can be kept for trimming and miscellaneous cutting of various materials such as rubberized hair, waddings, thin foam, etc., and a pair of **12in (305mm) cutting shears** for cover cutting.

Pinking shears and thread snips are of a more specialist nature. A pair of **pinking shears** is useful for the cutting of fine fabrics and for those types of cloth most likely to fray easily. The blades are serrated and make a zigzag cut, leaving the edge reasonably clean and less susceptible to fraying. A pair of **thread snips** is a tool used by the sewing machinist. It is lightweight and usually sprung, so that the blades are held open in readiness to trim thread or snip seams when necessary. The snips are often hung on a lace around the machinist's neck, or tucked into a pocket situated on the machine head. They are obviously much easier to handle at speed during sewing operations than a standard pair of shears. The five types are shown above and below.

1.1 Scissors and shears

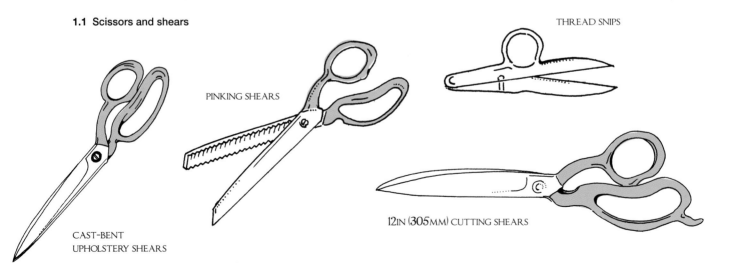

THREAD SNIPS

PINKING SHEARS

CAST-BENT
UPHOLSTERY SHEARS

12IN (305MM) CUTTING SHEARS

The **web strainer or stretcher** (*see* 1.2 below) has not changed in its design or shape since it was first made by early upholsterers. No other tool is quite so simple and yet so effective. The business of fixing and straining webbings is an essential skill that must be learned and perfected as early as possible by those entering the trade.

Webbed bases provide the foundation for both traditional and modern work. Good-quality beech, which has a close, straight grain with a natural resilience, is the accepted hardwood for web strainers. The timber should be between ⅝ and ¾in (16 and 20mm) thick, and the dowel peg should have a diameter of ⅝in (16mm). Most upholsterers use the standard bat-and-peg type of strainer, but with a little practice the other, simpler types are equally effective. In an emergency a short wood batten about 3in (75mm) wide will do the job quite well.

The spiked type of strainer is probably the least popular because of the damage that can be caused to the webbing itself during straining. This strainer is not suitable for pulling the woven polypropylene webbings used in modern production.

A pair of **metal strainers**, often called **iron hands**, with jaw widths of 2in (50mm) and 1in (25mm), is useful as a general straining or stretching tool. As they depend on the strength of the user's hand, they are limited for webbing applications, but they are often needed in hide work, and for tightening heavy canvases and sewn welts, etc. – in fact, in any situation where a cover requires a heavy pull beyond

1.3 Metal strainers or 'iron hands'

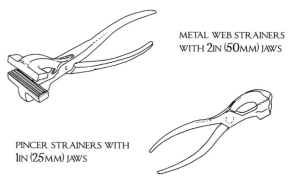

METAL WEB STRAINERS WITH 2IN (50MM) JAWS

PINCER STRAINERS WITH 1IN (25MM) JAWS

1.4 Ripping chisels and mallets

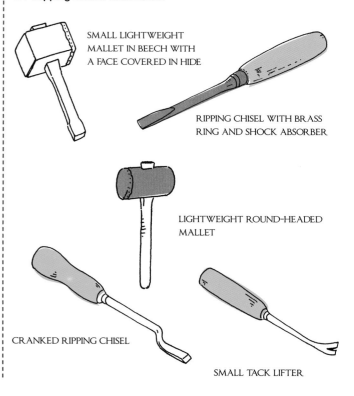

SMALL LIGHTWEIGHT MALLET IN BEECH WITH A FACE COVERED IN HIDE

RIPPING CHISEL WITH BRASS RING AND SHOCK ABSORBER

LIGHTWEIGHT ROUND-HEADED MALLET

CRANKED RIPPING CHISEL

SMALL TACK LIFTER

1.2 Wooden web strainers, best made from beech

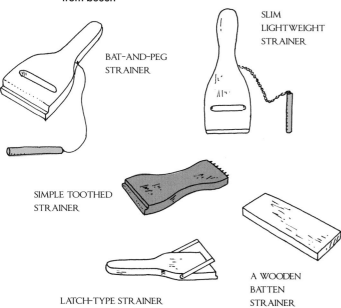

SLIM LIGHTWEIGHT STRAINER

BAT-AND-PEG STRAINER

SIMPLE TOOTHED STRAINER

LATCH-TYPE STRAINER

A WOODEN BATTEN STRAINER

normal tightness. Although expensive, the purchase of a pair of metal strainers will soon be justified, and they should be included in the tool kit as soon as possible (*see* 1.3).

The **ripping chisel**, or **ripper** (*see* 1.4), is designed specifically for the fast, easy removal of tacks and staples. It should be struck with the wooden mallet, and not with the tacking hammer. The most effective type of ripper, and the kind most used by the professional, is straight-bladed. This is a very strong tool with a heavy blade and a built-in shock absorber set in front of the brass ring where the blade is joined to the handle. Hickory and boxwood are used for the turned wood handle and will give good service if used with respect. The tip of the ripping-chisel blade is ground flat to a near-sharp chisel point. This will require grinding after long periods of heavy use, so that the tack heads and staples can be lifted easily with a sharp tap from the mallet.

Two other types of ripper or tack lifter are available. The **cranked-blade chisel** usually has a pear-shaped handle and a bevelled tip, and the **split-point tack lifter** is designed for removing tacks at a more gentle pace. There are occasions when all three types have their advantages. For example, when stripping close to show-wood in a rebate, the cranked type will provide better leverage and help to avoid unnecessary splitting at show-wood edges.

Heavy wooden **mallets** of the type employed by carpenters are not easy to use and will be found too cumbersome. The smaller lightweight versions, either round- or square-headed, are ideal and are easily handled for long periods. Stripping of upholstery work, often done many times before, can be very tiring and hard on the wrists and hands, so the tools should be as light as possible and the blades always good. Upholsterers' mallets are almost always made from good-grade beech, with chamfered edges and, most important, a comfortable handle. It is a habit of many craftsmen to cover one face of the mallet head with a piece of hide, which will preserve the face and reduce noise (*see* 1.4).

A selection of **trimming and cutting knives** will be found in any upholsterer's tool kit. Some have fixed blades which need to be regularly sharpened. Those with removable or retractable blades may be sharpened on an oilstone or the blades replaced when necessary. Whichever type is preferred, the tip of the blade will be used more than the rest of the blade and so will require constant attention. Although scissors are used regularly for the trimming of fabrics, when hide or vinyl-coated fabrics are being used the knife is more effective. This is particularly so when a clean, straight cut is required or an edge is to be thinned or skived. A **hide-skiving knife** has a curved bevelled edge on a strong, rigid blade. A sharp knife is invaluable when upholstery is being stripped from an old frame, and will often save unnecessary strain on scissors. A typical range of knives for trimming and skiving is shown below (*see* 1.5).

Now that the staple has become the common fixing medium for upholstery materials, a variety of **staple-lifting tools** is available. These are mostly produced by the staple-manufacturing companies, who have developed the lifters to assist the users of their products. However, because the holding properties of most frame-making hardwoods are so good, it is extremely difficult to lift and remove

1.5 Knives

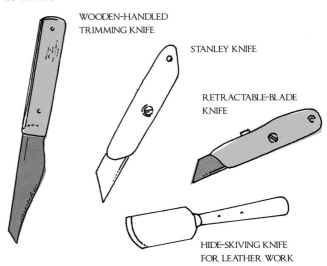

WOODEN-HANDLED TRIMMING KNIFE

STANLEY KNIFE

RETRACTABLE-BLADE KNIFE

HIDE-SKIVING KNIFE FOR LEATHER WORK

1.6 Three different types of staple lifters

1.7 Upholstery needles

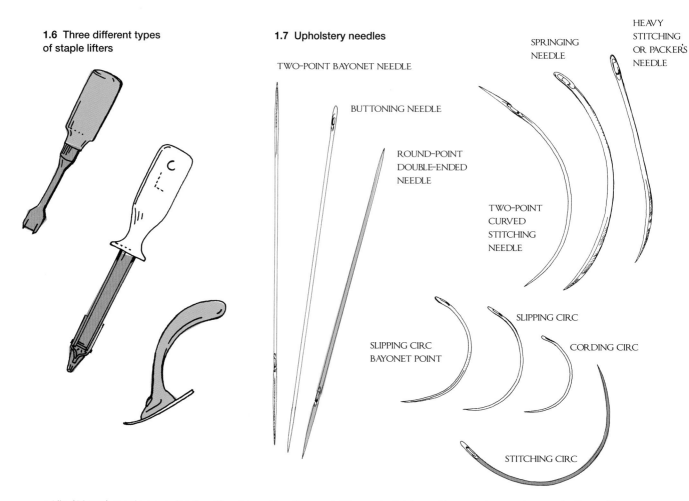

TWO-POINT BAYONET NEEDLE

BUTTONING NEEDLE

ROUND-POINT DOUBLE-ENDED NEEDLE

SPRINGING NEEDLE

HEAVY STITCHING OR PACKER'S NEEDLE

TWO-POINT CURVED STITCHING NEEDLE

SLIPPING CIRC

SLIPPING CIRC BAYONET POINT

CORDING CIRC

STITCHING CIRC

a ⅜in (10mm) staple completely without breaking it. If a staple lifter is used, a pair of small pincers will be needed to lift the bits of staple left in the rails. Those stubborn bits which break off low to the surface should be hammered back in. Some of the staple lifters available are shown above (see 1.6), all of which depend on the user's ability to dig the tool into the rail and under the staple crown. Most upholsterers would agree that they do not have time to remove all the staples in a chair one by one, so in practice covers are ripped off using the ripper and the lifter, then cleaned up and odd bits removed as quickly as possible.

A range of nine **upholstery needles** of various types and sizes provides the basic stitching and sewing equipment (see 1.7). Additional needles can be added if and when the work undertaken demands a greater range of sizes. The use of twine and thread to join and fix upholstery materials and to form stuffed shapes applies to traditional upholstery. In modern production work, such needles will be needed only for buttoning and the occasional small amount of slip stitching.

Three straight needles are shown above, starting with the 12in (305mm) **two-point bayonet needle**, 12- or 19-gauge, designed for edge stitching. A shorter **round-point**, **double-ended needle** 10in (255mm) by 13-gauge is for small stitched edges and scroll work.

The **buttoning needle** has a single round point and a large eye. It may be necessary to use a bayonet point for buttoning if particularly dense fillings or foams prove too difficult.

Curved and circular needles are peculiar to the upholstery trade. The length of a curved needle is measured around the curve and the gauge is the standard wire gauge (SWG) number indicating the thickness of the wire used to make the needle. The two heavy 8- or 10-gauge needles with four-sided bayonet points are **springing needles**. Their length is 5in (125mm), and they are used to sew in and fix springs and spring wires.

The **half-round, two-point needle** is excellent for edge stitching, close up to a show-wood rail, when a straight needle could be used only with great difficulty.

This is usually 12-gauge and 5 to 6in (125–150mm). The three **rounded-point circular needles** each have a different job. The longer 6in (150mm) 16-gauge is used with twine to produce stuffing ties and join hessian and scrims. The 3in (75mm) 18-gauge needle is a **slipping circ** used with slipping thread to close upholstery covers on chair outsides and cushions, etc. The smallest of the three needles is a **cording circ** and is used with strong thread to sew in cords and trimmings. Cording circs are usually 2½in (63mm), 18-gauge.

A 10in (255mm) **regulator** (*see* 1.8) is used to regulate and adjust fillings and manipulate covers. In fact, this tool has many uses, particularly in stitched-edge work. Sizes range from 8in (200mm) to 13in (330mm), and the smaller 8in size should be kept for small, lighter work.

The wooden **dolly stick** made from a length of beech is used to help fold and pleat fabrics and leather. The smooth, round point and flat spade-shaped end will be found generally kinder to materials than a steel tool. The stick is 7in (180mm) to 8in (200mm) long.

Skewers and **pins** have obvious uses as holding tools where temporary fixing of materials is needed prior to sewing or stitching. Pins are 1¼in (32mm) plated and skewers are usually 3in (75mm) or 4in (100mm).

A medium-sized **rasp** with a 10in (255mm) blade (*see* 1.9) is an essential woodworking tool for the upholsterer. Sharp edges on timber rails must be removed before upholstery begins, particularly on inside edges before webbings are applied. A well-rasped edge forming a chamfer is needed where scrim is to be turned in and tacked before making a stitched edge. (The rasp cuts only on the forward, pushing stroke and not when it is being drawn back.)

A pair of **pincers** is the standard tool for gripping and removing nails, pins and staple ends. It may also be used to cut soft wire and to lever out small nails of all kinds, using the claw at the end of the hand grip.

1.8 Other tools used in covering

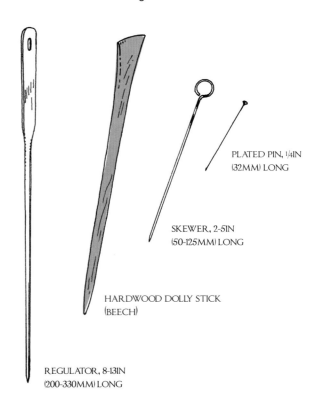

PLATED PIN, ¼IN (32MM) LONG

SKEWER, 2-5IN (50-125MM) LONG

HARDWOOD DOLLY STICK (BEECH)

REGULATOR, 8-13IN (200-330MM) LONG

1.9 Miscellaneous tools

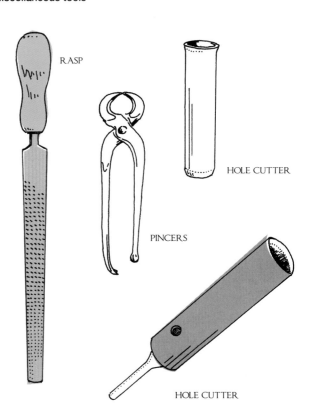

RASP

HOLE CUTTER

PINCERS

HOLE CUTTER

Two tube-shaped **hole cutters** are also illustrated on the previous page (*see* 1.9) and are used to punch or drill polyurethane foams in preparation for buttoning. One is simply a short length of 1in to 1¼in (25–32mm) steel tube which has been sharpened to a cutting edge at one end. This can be pushed into the foam by hand or hammered, depending on the thickness and density of the foam. The other type is designed for fitting to a power drill and is useful if a lot of foam drilling is done regularly. The power cutter is ground and sharpened from the inside, and has two holes drilled at the top end of the tube to allow air flow, and assist removal of the cut foam.

Tools and equipment for measuring and marking out materials (*see* 1.10) must be accurate and kept in good condition. They can be housed by hanging from hooks in a convenient place close to the cutting table. The **metre stick** is marked in metric measurements on one side and imperial on the other. It is the tool most used at the cutting table. This is complemented by

the **T-square** and a long straightedge. The T-square is used for marking across the width of the cutting table and will give accurate lines at 90° to the table edge. A **straightedge** of up to 6ft (2m) in length can be used for marking along the length of the roll or cutting table. A good example is the marking of piping strips which may be straight or bias-cut. A large **set square** made from plywood, usually at 60°, can be used with the T-square and provides a check for squareness at any time. A large pair of **compasses** should be included in the range of tools. Two types of **flexible measuring tape**, one steel and one linen, at least 4ft (1.2m) long, are needed for taking measurements from chairs, etc.

The following is a list of marking tools that are suitable for the surfaces that will be encountered.

- Tailor's crayon – most fabrics
- White stick chalk – vinyls, hides
- Soft pencil (4B) – hides and linings
- Felt pen – foams
- French dusting chalk – kraft paper stencils.

1.10 Marking and measuring tools

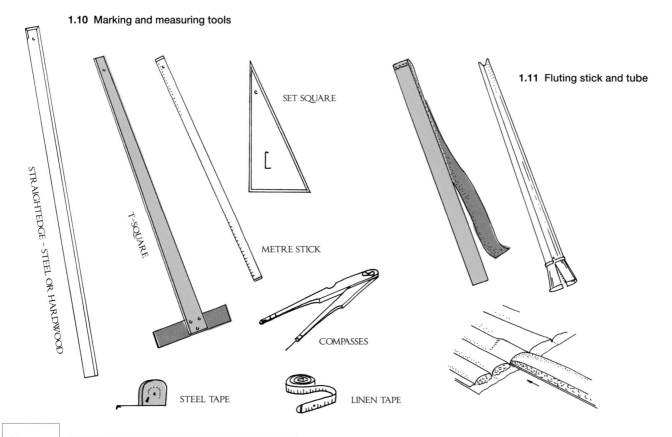

STRAIGHTEDGE - STEEL OR HARDWOOD

T-SQUARE

SET SQUARE

METRE STICK

COMPASSES

STEEL TAPE

LINEN TAPE

1.11 Fluting stick and tube

Flutes and channels in upholstered chair backs were traditionally hand-formed by stitching fabric down onto a base cloth or scrim in straight and curved lines. The section between the rows of stitching was then filled to form the flute before the next row of stitching was made. Using a **fluting stick or tube** (see 1.11), a complete panel can be machine-sewn to a pre-marked cloth base, then filled afterwards. The tube or stick both work in the same way; they are simply a means of inserting a length of thick filling such as cotton felt, curled hair and wadding, or a strip of foam wrapped in polyester into each separate flute. The length of filling is laid on the stick, the cloth strip pulled tightly down in the form of a sandwich and simply inserted into the open tube. The tool and the filling are then carefully pushed into the whole length of the flute and the tool removed, leaving the filling neatly in place.

The fluting stick is the more versatile of the two types because several widths of stick can be made very cheaply from ¼in (6mm) plywood and a matching strip of vinyl cloth fixed at one end. The ply strip must be well rounded at its edges and sanded to a fine, smooth finish. This ensures that the stick will slide easily into the flutes, and can be removed without disturbing the fillings. The width of the tool should be approximately ⅜in (10mm) less than the flute or channel to be filled. A set of fluting sticks of various widths can be kept and used or modified as and when they are needed. If the sticks are made at 3ft (1m) lengths, this will be long enough to deal with any normal-sized panels. Curved sticks to suit curved flutes are made and used in the same way.

The cutting and bending of spring wire is all part of the springing process. With the right tools (see 1.12), springs and spring units can be modified and adjusted to fit particular frame types. Edge wires for traditional and modern work can be cut and formed to suit a variety of spring edges and applications. The simplest and quickest way to cut wire of any type is with a pair of **bolt croppers**. These can be adjusted for jaw opening to deal with all gauges of wire, and make the cutting of high-carbon wires a quick and easy

1.12 Tools for working with wire

BOLT CROPPERS FOR CUTTING WIRE

A PIECE OF ½IN (13MM) TUBE FOR BENDING WIRE

A STRONG WIRE HOOK FOR PULLING AND TENSIONING SPRINGS AND DIAPHRAGMS

BENCH-MOUNTED WIRE FORMER

business. A short length of ½in (13mm) **steel tube** makes the bending of wire reasonably easy. The tube is simply slid along the wire to a point where the wire is to be bent, then by levering with the hands a right angle or radius can be formed. A bench vice will also do the job of holding the wire while a bend is formed, particularly when opposing angles are required. If necessary, the **bench-mounted wire former** is a device worth having. This works on a similar levering principle, while the wire is held between the metal stud and a small curved former.

A **strong wire hook** fixed to a wood handle is an extremely useful pulling tool, and can be easily made. The length of the wire hook will depend on the needs of the individual, but between 6 and 10in (150 and 250mm) is usual. The hook will assist with the stretching and insertion of tension springs, rubber platforms and spring units.

Of the variety of **hole punches** available, the adjustable six-way type is invaluable (see 1.13). This will cut neat holes from about ½²in (0.8mm) up to ¼in (6mm) in diameter in leather, plastics, fabrics, etc. There are occasions, however, when a single punch will be needed for cutting holes in the centre of patterns, templates or covers, or when making up a kraft paper stencil for repetition cutting of covers. Two or three sizes between ⅛in (3mm) and ⅜in (10mm) will be found adequate.

1.13 Hole punches, six-way and single

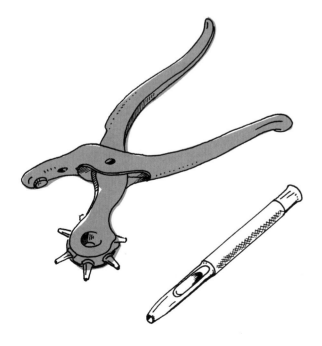

A typical set of **press-stud dies** with a **punch** for fitting press-stud fasteners to tapes, cushions and detachable upholstery components is shown in 1.14 The dies may be kept loose in a box or screwed down onto a board. The press fastener has many uses and provides a good detachable fixing between fabrics and leathers, and onto timber and metal frames.

Press studs are produced in four parts, two to form the top and two to form the base. These have to be punched together to fix them permanently to the covers being used.

The **spring balance** (*see* 1.15) can be kept handy for checking and weighing fillings of all types, both traditional and modern. To determine how much loose filling has been used in a particular job, a bag or sack of filling whose weight is known can be re-weighed at the end of the job. This gives an indication of the amount of filling used and also provides a form of stock control. Bags of new filling can also be checked for accuracy, and the density of polyurethane foam can be checked by weighing sample pieces and calculating the weight per cubic metre. It is also useful to know how much a particular cushion weighs after it has been filled with feather and down, or kapok, etc. The weights and dimensions of the cushions can be noted and such information used in the future. The weight of the filling may also be needed for costing. The spring balance should give kilograms and pounds so that comparisons can be made when necessary.

The **buttoning tool** (*see* 1.16) is especially designed for replacing upholstery buttons of all types that have come loose or broken out. The loose dart forms an anchor inside the upholstered chair and a button can be retied onto the twine using a slipknot. There are also many instances when this method of button fixing can be used on new work.

1.14 Press-stud dies and punch

1.15 Spring balance to weigh out fillings

1.16 Buttoning tool

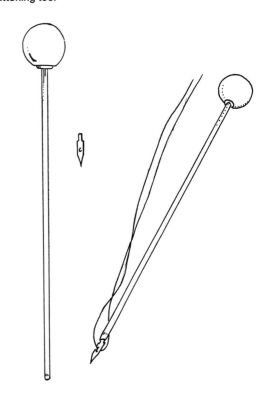

2. MATERIALS

The upholsterer uses a very wide range of materials for both traditional and modern work. Many of the materials one would expect to find in a chair made a hundred years ago have of course changed or been replaced – improvements in processing and the introduction of synthetics and new technology make this inevitable. But there is still a considerable demand for many of the good, naturally based materials such as webbings, fillings of animal or vegetable fibre, and woven cloths. The selection of materials and choosing what to use for a particular job is an important part of the upholstery work. Enjoy shopping around for the best and get into the habit of using both natural and synthetic materials where they are best suited to the project you are working on.

TACKS

Tacks are one of the basic essentials for all kinds of upholstery work. They are used for both temporary and permanent fixing, and are blued to keep them clean, distinctive and rust-free. If they should become exposed to damp for any length of time, however, they will rust. Upholstery tacks are selected by their size for different uses, and generally it is true that the larger sizes are for heavy work, such as fixing hessians, webbings, and lashing cords. The smaller sizes are kept particularly for fixing scrim, calico and upholstery fabrics.

There are two grades of tack: fine and improved. The improved types have a larger head than the fine grade. The different leg lengths are available in both grades. It is not necessary to have all the sizes in both fine and improved, but a useful selection would be: ⅝in (15mm) improved, ½in (13mm) fine, ⅜in (10mm) fine and ¼in (6mm) fine. These four will be quite adequate for most types of upholstery work. Some ½in (13mm) improved could be added to the list as a strong tack for general and light webbing work. For very heavy fixings and for lashing work with springs and so on, ⅝in (15mm) improved are used. As a general rule, it is a good idea to keep the tack sizes to the smaller grades and sizes wherever possible.

Hammering in large tacks unnecessarily is noisy and tiring, and will cause damage, so choose fine tacks in the shorter lengths for most general fixings, and keep the improved and longer lengths for the occasional heavy applications. See 2.0 for examples of tack size and suitable spacing.

GIMP PINS

A gimp pin is a fine-cut steel tack with a very small head that is painted in a variety of colours. Gimp pins are used as a finishing tack to fix upholstery fabrics and braids or gimps, and as a first fixing before decorative nailing and banding. There are two leg lengths: ⅜in and ½in (10mm and 13mm).

Use gimp pins instead of tacks where timber rails are delicate and where decorative edges are to be trimmed. Keep a small stock of both lengths in several different colours. Fawn, black and white are the most common, while red green and blue are also available.

STAPLES

The staple is an alternative fixing used in upholstery and has to be fired into a frame with a stapler or staple gun. The staple is a quick, efficient and clean method of fixing materials to a timber frame. Once fired in, however, a staple is more difficult to remove than a tack. Staple fixings can be less intrusive and damaging, particularly when a frame is old or delicate, and not able to cope with repeated hammering. Ideally use tacks as a temporary fixing and to set linings and covers in place. When shaping and stretching is complete and there is no need for further adjustment, then use the staple as a permanent finish.

STAPLE SIZES

The width of a staple is called the crown width, and this may vary from one manufacturer to another. The leg lengths available for upholstery are between ⅛in and ⅝in (3mm and 16mm). Use ⅛–¼in (3–6mm) for fine shallow surfaces, ⅜in (10mm) for most average fixings and ½–⅝in (13–16mm) for stronger heavy applications, for example, when working with webbing.

WEBBING

Tightly stretched strips of webbing have been used to support upholstered seating for around 300 years. Basically we still use the same system today, even though the raw materials and the structure of webbings have developed and improved in many ways. There are now many variations to suit the different methods of furniture manufacture, and the amount of support, both firm and flexible, required of a chair seat.

Nylon, polypropylene, synthetic rubbers, metals, cotton, jute and linen are all used in the making of webbings for upholstery. Webbings for upholstery

2.0 Some examples showing the tack size and the adequate tack spacing

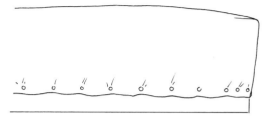

⅜in (10mm) fine tacks 1in (25mm) apart for calico

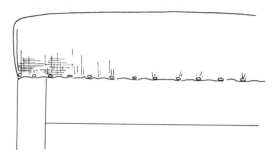

¼in (6mm) and ⅜in (10mm) fine tacks for fixing scrim

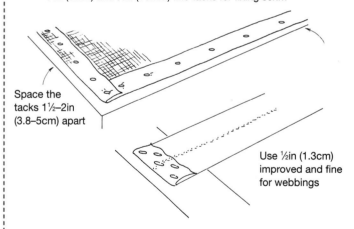

Space the tacks 1½–2in (3.8–5cm) apart

Use ½in (1.3cm) improved and fine for webbings

are mostly 2in (5cm) wide, but in continental Europe they tend to be a little wider, up to 3½in (9cm). For traditional upholstery work, the conventional 2in (5cm) black and white, brown and white and all brown are used. These are all made from natural raw materials, but they often have a small percentage of synthetic fibre added for extra strength.

Modern upholstery has changed and developed dramatically in recent years, and webbings, when they are used, are mostly manufactured blends and compositions of materials such as nylon, metals and rubbers. Products such as elastic webbing, rubber webbing and woven polypropylene webbing are well suited to the design and manufacture of the modern chair.

There are two versions of what is known as English webbing: the black and white, and the brown and white. These are both excellent and easily available. The alternatives are the 10lb (4.5kg) and 12lb (5.5kg) all-brown webs, made from 100% jute and sold in their natural colours. The two types, English and jute, are distinguished by their weave patterns, which are herringbone twill and plain weave.

Black bottom lining

A fine plain woven lining cloth, usually dyed black and used as a finishing cover or dust cover on the underside of chairs and settees. As the name suggests, a bottom lining is used to provide a neat finish and a dust cover under seats. The edges of the lining are always turned in and neatly tacked or stapled along the centre of the rails, and never too near to the outer edge. Black linings are functional and should never be seen. A 10oz (305g) hessian can also be used as an under-cover when a black cloth is not available. Occasionally a lining of this type is used to line a seat by fixing it on top of the rails before upholstery begins. This type of finish is well suited to small unsprung occasional chairs and dining chairs.

Calico

A fine unbleached white cotton cloth used in upholstery as a lining or first covering over second stuffings. It is good practice to complete a piece of upholstery in calico, before the final or top cover is applied. A calico lining can be very tightly stretched and allows precise shaping, so that upholstery fabrics, which may sometimes be delicate, can be pulled down and fixed with care. Calico will take much of

the initial strain and will also support the top covering, giving it a good appearance and at the same time prolonging its life. A calico lining will also allow the beginner to experiment and to test difficult cutting operations at corners and around frame supports, legs, arms and so on.

Once a calico cover is in place it can be used as a marking surface where features and details are to be built into the upholstery design, for example, pull-ins, tufting and shallow fluting. Collars around arms and piped joints can also be accurately positioned and drawn before the main covering stage. Calico covers are seldom turned in at their edges, but are simply pulled down and tacked on to rail faces before being trimmed close to the tack line.

Cambric

A fine close-weave all-cotton fabric with a very smooth surface, which is usually glazed. Cambric is an excellent lining cloth that is made feather-proof by a waxing process. It has a luxurious feel and is used principally as a cushion interior lining for feather and down fillings.

The cloth works well and can be cut and sewn with good accuracy. It is available in 36in (90cm), 48in (122cm) and 72in (180cm) widths. When making up cambric into cushion cases, the shiny side of the cloth should be to the inside or filling side to help the movement of the fillings.

Ticking

Ticking is a strong twill weave fabric, traditionally woven from white cotton with a narrow black stripe in the warp direction. It is proof against fibrous filling materials such as feathers, hair, flocks and kapok. Tickings are available in a variety of widths and are also produced as soft furnishing fabrics in both colour stripe and woven patterns for bedding and upholstery.

DUCK

A heavyweight version of calico usually 10oz or 15oz (305gm and 458gm). Cotton duck is used as a support material in modern upholstery and in outdoor seating, such as deckchairs. It cuts and works well and is generally plain weave. Duck is available in 39in (1m), 59in (1.5m) and 79in (2m) widths.

STOCKINETTE

A single jersey knitted fabric made from rayon and other synthetic yarns, stockinette is made in a continuous sock and will stretch to several times its relaxed size.

A length of stockinette is cut from the roll and stretched over foams, cushion interiors and synthetic fibre fillings. It is basically a very soft lightweight lining used to contain and hold in place, and make handling easier.

Use stockinette linings over foams and foam/fibre interiors, before covering with upholstery fabric. The cut ends are sealed by hand-stitching, overlocking or heat sealing.

UPHOLSTERY SCRIM

Scrim cloths are used for shaping work over first stuffings in traditional upholstery. They can be easily manipulated and are generally finer in weave and yarn than a hessian. Jute yarns are used to weave and produce 6oz (185g) and 9oz (290g) hessian scrims, 72in (183cm) wide.

Linen scrims are made from 100% linen (flax) yarns and are considered to be the best for fine shape work and edge making in upholstery. However, they are noticeably more expensive and are available only in 36in (90cm) widths. For general edge work, a 9oz (290g) hessian scrim gives a very satisfactory result.

HESSIAN

A strong, coarse plain woven cloth made from 100% jute and used in upholstery as a supporting base cloth. Hessians are bought by the metre length and are available in several different widths, for example, 30in (76cm), 36in (90cm), 40in (101.5cm) and 72in (183cm). The quality of a hessian is measured by the weight of a square metre in ounces or grams. Typical weights for upholstery work are: 7½oz (229g), 10oz (305g), 12oz (366g), 15oz (458g).

A medium weight ideal for general lining work is 10oz (305g) hessian, while 12oz (366g) is recommended as a minimum weight over sprung upholstery in backs and seats. A large fully sprung seat should be lined with 15oz (452g) hessian (sometimes referred to as tarpaulin).

TWINES AND CORDS

Strong twines and cord are used for tying, stitching and lashing in all kinds of upholstery work. Mattress twines, as they are called, are used for all types of stitch work, and are made from pure linen. Twine numbers 3, 4 and 5 are the thicknesses most used in traditional work. No. 3 is ideal for edge stitching and the heavier No. 5 for the more general tying and stitching.

Lashing cords, called laid cords, are the very strong heavy cords used to lash and hold springs in place, in chair seats and backs. Made from hemp, laid cords are specifically designed to do a tough job and remain stable under tension.

SLIPPING THREADS

A strong linen stitching thread used for the hand stitching and closing of upholstery covering fabrics. These threads are bought in skeins or small reels in a variety of different colours. Keep a stock of a few colours. Your selection should include 'drab' (a muddy brown), black and some white. When slip stitching, the thread is virtually invisible, and so drab will do for use with most fabric colours. However, an additional small selection of colours will always ensure that you are able to get the nearest possible match.

Slipping threads are lightly waxed which keeps them strong and twist-free, and gives the thread grip in order to produce a tight and positive handmade join.

2.1 A selection of plaited slipping thread

SPRINGS AND FLEXIBLE WEBBINGS

The springs used for traditional upholstery are double cone compression springs (see 2.2). They are waisted at their centres and have an hourglass shape. There is a good range of sizes available from 3in (7.5cm) up to 9in (23cm) high and with wire gauges or thicknesses (swg) from 14swg down to 8swg. The higher the gauge number, the finer the wire will be, and so the softer the spring will be.

Spring wires used for seats tend to be from 8swg up to 10swg, and those used in chair-back supports and chair-arm upholstery will generally be in the range 11 to 14swg wires. Some seat springs are available in half sizes, for example, 9½swg and 10½swg. Below are some spring sizes and some recommended uses for each.

4in (10cm) x 9swg	for stools and firm chair-seat platforms, under cushions
5in (12.5cm) x 9½swg	for firm chair seats and fully sprung armchairs
5in (12.5cm) x 9swg	as above
6in (15cm) x 9½swg	for easy chairs and wing chairs, nursing chairs and sewing chairs
6in (15cm) x 10swg	for fully sprung arm chairs and spring edge seats

TENSION SPRINGS

Tension springs are a very different type of upholstery spring, designed for use in the modern chair. These were first introduced in the 1950s in seating and were well suited to the more lightweight, less deep-upholstered chairs of the time. The close-coiled cable spring and the zigzag wire spring are both tension springs and have been used in large quantities during the second half of the twentieth century. They are both used as lateral suspension and are stretched under tension across a chair seat or back frame.

2.2 The double cone compression spring, sold in bundles of 50

FLEXIBLE WEBBINGS

Flexible webbings are available as rubber webbings or as elastic webbings with various proprietary fixings. Both of these flexible webbings are available in roll lengths that can be fixed and cut as desired onto chair frames. Depending on the type of webbing chosen, tensioning may be from as low as 7.5% or as high as 90%. Providing coverage is at around 50% of the area to be sprung – the gap between the webs is equal to the width of the webbing – then these types of webbing produce a very good suspension for modern chair seats and backs. They are also very well suited to both timber and tubular steel frame constructions.

EDGE ROLL AND DUG ROLL

Edge rolls are available in ready-to-use form, with or without a flange for fixing. Sizes range from ⅜in (10mm) up to 1³⁄₁₆in (30mm) diameter. This handy product is used to upholster along seat, arm and chair-back rail edges, where a quickly applied soft roll is required. It eliminates the need for a more complex edging, more usual in traditional work. Edge roll or dug roll is generally made from recycled paper or a firm extruded plastic foam, and can be cut, stapled or tacked, either directly onto a chair frame or neatly rolled up in a hessian lining cloth.

FILLINGS

Coir or coconut fibre is bought as black-dyed or undyed ginger fibre and sold by the kilogram or pound. This is an ideal filling for use as a first stuffing in traditional upholstery, particularly where a stitched edge is to be built in sprung or unsprung seating. Coir is an excellent vegetable filling which has been curled during processing and usually made fire retardant.

FILLINGS

Coir (coconut)	ginger and dyed	1st stuffing
Hair	grey curled hair	1st and 2nd stuffings
	white combings	1st and 2nd stuffings
	horsehair	1st and 2nd stuffing
	cashmere	2nd stuffing
Flax	undyed	1st stuffing
Skin wadding	cotton	top stuffing
Polyester wadding	Dacron or Terylene	topping
Cotton felt		2nd stuffing and topping
Wool felt		2nd stuffing and topping
Rubberized hair	sheet	soft 1st stuffing
Foams	sheet	general

ANIMAL HAIR

One of the best and most versatile upholstery fillings, which has its uses in both traditional and modern upholstery and bedding, is animal hair. Curled animal hair is resilient, warm and inherently fire-resistant.

Hair fillings are available in various grades and types. Grey curled hair is the most popular and is a blend of pig, cow and horse mane and tail. White combings from cow tails is another good grade and is often superior in length and curl. Pure horsehair is a superior quality filling, chosen for its excellent curl, resilience and length. It is generally the most expensive of the hair fillings.

POLYESTER WADDING

Polyester wadding is available in several thicknesses or weights, and in a number of different widths. These waddings are resilient, soft and warm, and are used in all kinds of upholstered surfaces. A roll of 162ft (50m) by 27in (68cm) wide in 2oz (70g) or 4oz (135g) weight is ideal stock for most applications. It is easily cut, laminated, rolled or folded to any thickness, and can be glued or stapled in place when necessary. The resilience and flexibility of polyester waddings make them the upholsterer's best friend. They provide good support and good stretch around curving surfaces, as well as immediately under covering fabrics.

They are now used universally over all foam fillings to provide a soft flexible barrier between foam and fabric covering. Two-ounce (70g) wadding has a thickness of about ¼in (6mm) and can be stretched by about 30% in any direction without breaking. This feature makes it ideal as an upholstery medium and will help to produce a good line and a warm soft feel to a surface covering.

SKIN WADDING

Skin wadding is used very extensively in traditional work as a topping or final stuffing layer, either before calico covering or after, or both. The paperlike surface acts as a barrier that prevents hair fillings from penetrating through linings and covers.

Skin waddings are purchased in small rolls of 10 or 20m lengths which are 18in (457mm) wide. The wadding can be split or opened by parting the thickness to give a very thin layer 36in (914mm) wide. When split, several layers are used together to form a good hairproof topping.

These waddings are very versatile and can be used layered up to various thicknesses, rolled or folded for borders or for fluting work. The outside coverings on chairs, sofas and so on are usually lined with skin waddings.

2.3 Polyester fibre, cotton felt and skin wadding

CASHMERE

A fine goat hair which makes an excellent second stuffing for high-quality traditional upholstery, cashmere is usually bought as a hair-pad needled into a hessian base, and is sold by the roll or per metre. The hair can easily be pulled out and separated from its hessian cloth base, then teased ready for use as a loose filling.

Its high cost usually means that it tends to be reserved for work of the highest quality, for example, period chairs with unsprung seats and delicate chairback panels. It is also ideal as a top stuffing in hair-filled squabs and cushions.

RUBBERIZED HAIR

This is a processed filling bought in sheet form ready for use. Sheets are usually 1in (25mm) thick and measure about 78in x 39in (2m x 1m). It is a very useful and adaptable filling made from a blend of grey curled hair and rubber compounds.

Rubberized hair can be cut easily with scissors, shaped and chamfered, or layered and laminated to various thicknesses required. It bonds well with spray adhesive and can also be fixed in place with tacks and staples. It has good resilience and is ideal for use in bed headboards and chairbacks and arms as a first stuffing with a thin layer of loose hair and some cotton or wool felt over as a topping. When laminated up to 5cm (2in) or 7.5cm (3in) thick rubberized hair is an excellent base filling for attaching deep buttoning to, particularly in combination with an overlay or topping of white cotton felt.

COTTON FELT AND WOOL FELT

As the name 'felt' suggests, these soft fillings are much heavier and thicker than waddings. New cotton and reclaimed wool are felted into useable fillings in roll form, about 1in (25mm) thickness. A roll contains around 22 yards (20m), usually 27in (68cm) wide.

There are two weights or thicknesses available, 2½oz (83g) and 4oz (135g) per square foot. Cotton felts are made from pure new cotton and are a little more expensive than the wool felts, but well worth the extra cost.

Both of these fillings are supported on soft paper, which is removed as the felt is unrolled and applied. The paper separates the layers and also facilitates handling. Felts can be torn across the roll width, but need to be cut along their length. Edges can be feathered to assist with shaping, by picking and thinning.

UPHOLSTERY FOAMS

Upholstery foam is a cellular plastic upholstery filling which is made from polyurethane, an oil-based product. Foams can be purchased in sheet form at any thickness from ¼in (6mm) up to 4in (10cm). Alternatively, foams are cut and supplied in cushion-size shapes to almost any dimension required. A pattern or template will be needed for shapes or profiles that have varying thickness. At thicknesses above 8in (20cm), large pieces of foam are referred to as blocks. For example, a block or a cube 20in x 20in x 12in (51cm x 51cm x 30cm) can be cut and supplied to those measurements, or a circular block 20in radius x 12in (51cm x 30cm) will require a template as a cutting guide.

Upholstery foams are produced combustion-modified (CM) to various densities and hardness. High-density foams are the most expensive and can be made in a range of different hardnesses. The hardness of a foam is usually referred to as the 'feel'. Here are some typical foam types and their recommended uses. Most foam manufacturers and suppliers will recommend the most suitable for a particular end use.

CM	Combustion-modified or fire-retardant to different levels or specifications, e.g. domestic use or public use
HR	High resilience
CHIPFOAM	Reconstituted CM foam
PU	Polyurethane
PE	Polyether (conventional foam)

Examples:

Grade	Colour	Density range	Hardness range	Class of use
CMHR25s	White	23–26	50–75	A
CMHR35	Green	38–42	115–150	S
CMHR40h	Blue	38–42	155–190	S
CMHR50	White	48–52	195–235	V

Foam classification (class of use) is the performance of the foam under load-bearing conditions.

Class	Type of class	Recommended application
X	Extremely severe	Heavy-duty seating
V	Very severe	Commercial vehicle seats
S	Severe	Domestic seats and mattresses
A	Average	Chair backs and arm rests
L	Light	Padding, cushions, pillows

3. FABRICS AND TRIMMINGS

Choosing and using furnishing fabrics and trimmings is an exciting part of the craft of upholstery. An ordinary and very plain piece can be made to look extremely impressive when a good fabric of the right colour with an interesting texture is used. However if a chair, sofa or screen, for example, has a strong style or is heavily carved then a relatively plain fabric will enhance the design. Buy the best materials that can be afforded and are available to you – this approach will show in your work and help you to produce upholstery of good quality – and enjoy the freedom to work with fabrics and coverings in both a functional and decorative way.

UPHOLSTERY FABRICS

If you take a close look at a roll of upholstery fabric, then take a tape measure and check the width of the roll – that is, from one selvedge across to the other – it will be somewhere between 51in and 57in (130cm and 145cm). This is about average and is a familiar width to anyone buying and using fabrics for upholstery.

The width of a fabric is set by the manufacturing process of weaving. A fabric is created by weaving two basic sets of yarns together: the weft yarns, which are those running across or side to side, and the warp yarns, which are those running down the length of the fabric, or the roll. These are bought by the metre or yard, and once cut, they are referred to as cut lengths.

Furnishing fabrics are generally grouped into three categories: curtaining, loose covers and fixed upholstery. Those made for upholstery will mainly be more robust and heavier in weight. They need to be fit for the purpose and be capable of being cut and sewn, stretched and fixed, as well as having good resistance to wear and tear.

Today we demand clear information about the products that we buy, and fabrics are no exception. Look for the labelling on a fabric and check the fibre content, the width of the fabric in centimetres or inches, its suitability for use, the colourways available, the pattern repeat size, and of course, the price per metre or yard. Ask for as much information as possible about the fabric that you intend to buy and always buy just a little more than you actually need. As soon as possible after purchase, check the fabric closely yourself, making sure that it is the length that you intended, the condition is good and there are no surface faults. Most suppliers will be happy to replace a faulty piece, providing you have not cut into it and that you have the original receipt.

There is a vast range of light, medium and heavy coverings that are eminently suitable for upholstery use. A large percentage of these contain natural fibres, which are frequently blended with synthetics to create the properties required for the job. Wool, cotton and linen are often blended with rayon, nylon or acrylics to give the best of both worlds.

Over the long history of the upholstery textile, styles, colourings and textures have changed, developed, and moved in and out of fashion. On the facing page is an interesting sample of the type of fabric that has been used to furnish chairs and sofas since the beginning of the seventeenth century.

A Width
B Warp yarns
C Weft yarns
D Bias direction
E Selvedge
F Half width
G Pattern repeat
H Length or cut length

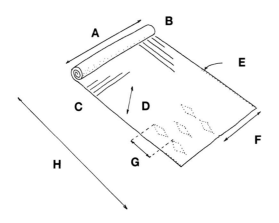

3.0 A typical upholstery cover/fabric

Early 17th century	Indian cottons, Turkish work, plain wool cloths
Late 17th century	velvets, silk brocade, leathers
Early 18th century	embroidery work, damask, chintz
Late 18th century	French and English tapestry, haircloth
Early 19th century	brocades, silk damask, patterned velour
Late 19th century	wool plush, embossed leather, printed cottons
Early 20th century	leathercloths, printed unions, stylized tapestry
Late 20th century	moquette, tweeds, synthetic velvets, chenille

TAKING CARE OF YOUR UPHOLSTERY FABRICS

Avoid folding a fabric or a leather, either before or after cutting. Large or small pieces should be rolled and laid on a flat surface if left for any length of time. Velvets, hides and leathercloths are particularly vulnerable to permanent creasing by folding.

The fabric on a piece of upholstered furniture is usually the most expensive part and may well exceed the value of all the other materials. Use a dust cover when work is not in progress on a piece of work that is partially covered with fabric or completed. Regular soft brushing or gentle vacuum cleaning will keep covers in good condition. Fabrics are weakened by dust and grit. Most fabric suppliers grade their range of covers for wear. The wearing qualities of upholstery fabrics vary enormously, depending on the strength of the yarn and the weaving technique used. Pile fabrics such as velvet and chenille may flatten when people sit on them. This is mostly inevitable and does not affect the durability of the fabric.

Leather will age and crease attractively, but will need cleaning from time to time. Leather suppliers will be happy to advise about cleaning, but basically, after removing dust, the surface should simply be wiped with a cloth that has been dampened with a very mild soap.

Cushions should be plumped and rotated to keep furniture looking fresh and good, and to spread the wear. Fabrics are damaged by direct heat and strong sunlight, which weakens fibres and fades the colours. Loose threads should never be cut or pulled, but carefully threaded and needled back into the upholstery.

Spillages and stains need to be dealt with quickly, but make sure you don't use anything wetter than a damp cloth. Soaking an upholstery fabric can leave a permanent mark or cause puckering and damage to the interior.

Fabric work and trimming

Techniques such as pleating, ruching and buttoning are widely used and have become recognized work methods based on historic development. Each in its way produces the surface detail and design that gives a piece of upholstered furniture its distinct style or finish.

Many of these decorative techniques are simply fine details used to trim and enhance as expressions of the craft. You should allow yourself to be influenced by the origin of a piece, or by a desire to simplify or enhance an original style. Although much of the work we do is concerned with chairs and seating of various kinds, the opportunity is always there to use other techniques. Wall coverings, upholstered screens, ottomans and bed upholstery are good examples of how inventive fabric work and trimming methods can produce fascinating results.

Measuring and estimating fabric quantities

Use a tape measure to obtain the length and width of all the fabric parts you will need. Label the parts and record a set of measurements for each piece of fabric. Assume the fabric width will be average, for example, 49in to 55in (124.5cm to 140cm), unless you already have the fabric to hand. Draw a sketch plan, and lay out all the cover parts onto your plan of the cover.

If the larger parts, such as the inside back or the seat panel, are wider than half the width of the fabric, it is likely that the next piece in the layout will have to be cut from below, rather than at the side of the first. Always centre the main pieces to be cut by cutting a notch or by putting in a pin and aligning these with the centre of any pattern or stripe. Remember that inside back pieces, outside back pieces and seats on chairs have to match up and have the same centre line.

Most of the smaller parts where two are required, such as arm pads or facings, can be cut as pairs, which simply means that they will be mirror images, and in most cases will be identical.

Plain coverings are generally easier to deal with and are usually more economical to use. Pile fabrics, such as velvets or velours, although they are plain

3.1 The lay of a cover on an easy chair

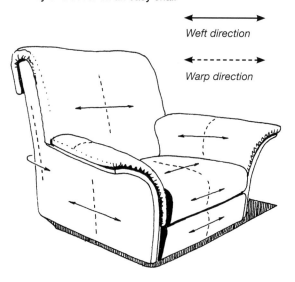

Weft direction

Warp direction

in appearance, have their own set of rules for cutting. They have a pile surface which has a lay or a nap, and this will make the fabric appear dark when viewed from one direction and much lighter when viewed from another. This is often referred to as shading. When pile fabrics are cut and placed on a chair, the pile should always brush down and feel smooth. A chair seat will follow on from the back and will brush forwards, feeling smooth to the touch when the hand or fingers are brushed from the back of the seat towards the front. All these points have to be considered when fabrics are being chosen, and when they are being cut and prepared to be used for upholstery.

Another useful tip is that all upholstery fabrics are positioned and fixed onto a chair with the weft yarns (horizontal yarns) running parallel to the floor (*see* 3.1). This applies equally to all the different parts and on any design of chair. Two notable exceptions are railroaded fabrics and horsehair fabrics. The majority of upholstery fabrics, however, are designed and made in the conventional way. That is, the warp yarns run vertically and are the main structure of the fabric, and the weft yarns, running horizontally, form the pattern and the surface texture.

When measurements are recorded before cover cutting (*see* 3.2), always try to write the length measurement first, followed by the width. When a sketch plan is completed and all the parts required are drawn, the length measurements can then be totalled to give the overall requirement in metres or yards. Whenever possible the quantity is rounded up to the nearest whole metre or yard. If a fabric has a large pattern or motif the length of the pattern repeat is also added to the total. This helps to ensure that enough of the pattern design is available for the whole project.

A certain amount of waste is inevitable when upholstery fabrics are being cut; however, many of the waste pieces will be used up for smaller parts and also for pipings, fly pieces and sometimes buttons.

3.2 Measuring a wing chair for a cover

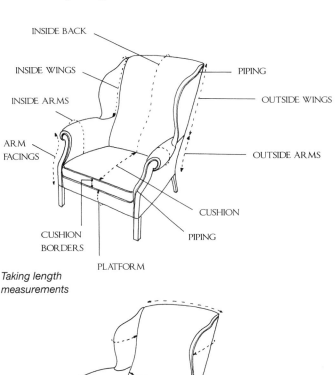

Taking length measurements

Taking width measurements, most of which can be paired on the cutting plan

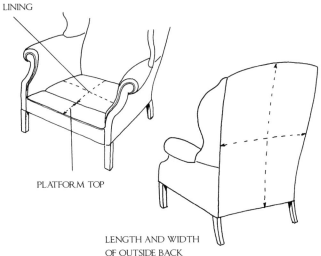

4. BASIC TECHNIQUES

From the middle of the seventeenth century, the upholstery of chairs and seating, as well as occasional furniture and bedding, took on a more structured form. The building and filling of padded areas to provide comfort slowly developed into the craft that we now know as upholstery. Contributions and influences from European craftsmen changed the way in which various natural materials and fillings were used and shaped to produce what is known as stitched-edge upholstery.

These basic skills and techniques, which have been handed down for generations, provide us with an essential grounding in the art of upholstery. They need to be practised and repeated, so that a series of skills and a basic knowledge is at your command. This chapter can be used as a reference and a useful reminder as you deal with each different project that needs new upholstery or reupholstery.

Watching an upholsterer at work, whenever there is an opportunity, is another valuable way in which the basics can be appreciated. A great deal can also be learned from dismantling old pieces of upholstered furniture, providing that it is done with care and in the correct sequence. This is a good opportunity to make some notes and take photographs as a reminder of the order of assembly.

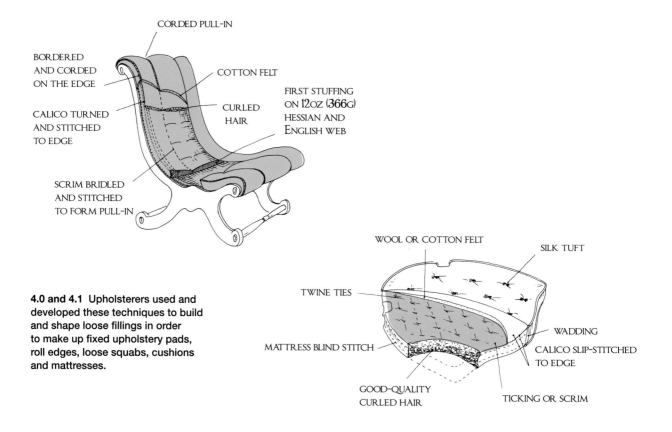

CORDED PULL-IN

BORDERED AND CORDED ON THE EDGE

COTTON FELT

CALICO TURNED AND STITCHED TO EDGE

CURLED HAIR

FIRST STUFFING ON 12oz (366g) HESSIAN AND ENGLISH WEB

SCRIM BRIDLED AND STITCHED TO FORM PULL-IN

WOOL OR COTTON FELT

SILK TUFT

TWINE TIES

WADDING

MATTRESS BLIND STITCH

CALICO SLIP-STITCHED TO EDGE

GOOD-QUALITY CURLED HAIR

TICKING OR SCRIM

4.0 and 4.1 Upholsterers used and developed these techniques to build and shape loose fillings in order to make up fixed upholstery pads, roll edges, loose squabs, cushions and mattresses.

WEBS AND WEBBING

Webbings are the materials that are used to support most types of basic upholstery. These are fixed using a web strainer or stretcher, to produce a well-tensioned base.

Some different treatments and variations of webbing patterns are shown in 4.2 and 4.3. The different patterns are chosen to suit different frame sizes and shapes. For example, a seat with curving rails will have a different weave arrangement to a seat with straight rails. Similarly, a chair or stool with a round seat frame can be given a different layout or treatment to a seat with a square frame. There are many variations, and the more pieces of upholstery that you discover, the more experience will be gained.

4.2 Uses of webbing

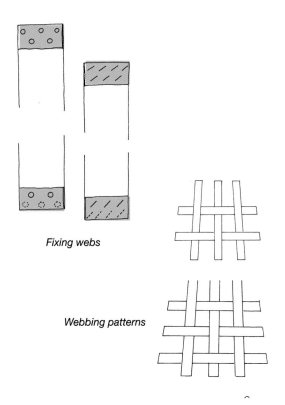

Fixing webs

Webbing patterns

4.3 Uses of webbing

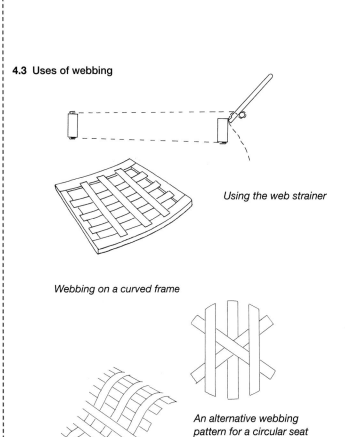

Using the web strainer

Webbing on a curved frame

An alternative webbing pattern for a circular seat

Treatment of webbing on a scroll end or arm

Supporting the long cross webs over a centre stretcher rail on a settee

4.4 The basic web fixing method is shown below

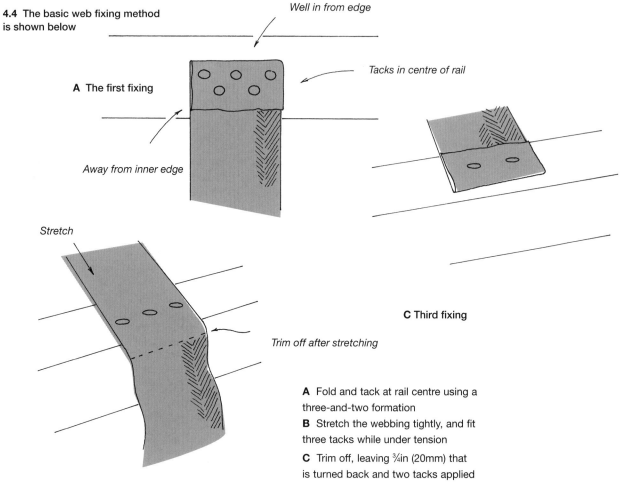

Well in from edge

A The first fixing

Tacks in centre of rail

Away from inner edge

Stretch

C Third fixing

Trim off after stretching

A Fold and tack at rail centre using a three-and-two formation
B Stretch the webbing tightly, and fit three tacks while under tension
C Trim off, leaving ¾in (20mm) that is turned back and two tacks applied

B Second fixing and trimming

It is better to use too much webbing than not enough, and spacing of the webbing should at least be adequate for the job that it will perform. A good general formula that will suit most types of work is to fix webs at 5in (12.5cm) centres, or in the case of seats, where most strain is likely, fix the webbing with spaces equal to the width of the webbing, for example 2in (5cm).

Other than in very lightweight work, a minimum tack size of ½in (13mm) fine or improved should be used. Where stapling is preferred then ½in and ⅜in (13mm x 10mm) should be used for fixing, the longer staple being used for frames where the timber is old and already full of tack holes.

LINING UP IN HESSIAN

Hessian is the first covering over webbing where a piece of work is simply top-stuffed and is unsprung. In this case the hessian used is 10oz (305g) or 12oz (366g) weight and is pulled taut by hand tightly in all directions, ⅜in (10mm) fine or improved tacks are used in most cases. Loose seats, top-stuffed seats, arms and wings are lined with hessian in this way.

When a seat or sometimes a chair back is sprung then the hessian lining follows after the springs have been fitted. A 12oz (366g) or tarpaulin-weight hessian is used over spring work because of the extra amount of movement and wear and tear that is likely in a sprung foundation.

Lightweight hessians such as 7oz (216g) and 10oz (305g) are adequate for lining up the outside areas of chairs. These support coverings and waddings when, for example, outside upholstery fabrics are being applied and finished off (*see* 4.5).

4.5 Lining the outside of a chair

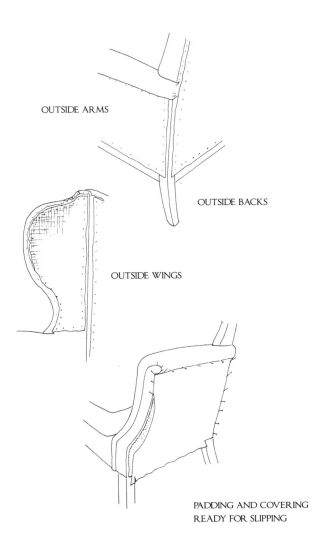

OUTSIDE ARMS

OUTSIDE BACKS

OUTSIDE WINGS

PADDING AND COVERING
READY FOR SLIPPING

KNOTS AND TWINES

Upholstery twines are relatively fine and are graded as sizes 1 to 5, size number 1 being the finest. Size number 5 is a heavy twine used principally for tying in springs and some lightweight lashing work, and also for buttoning. Size number 3 is a good weight for stitching and the forming of stitched edges. When an exceptionally strong twine is needed for tufting and buttoning, a yellow nylon twine can be used, especially where there is likely to be movement or strain.

4.6 Twines and threads

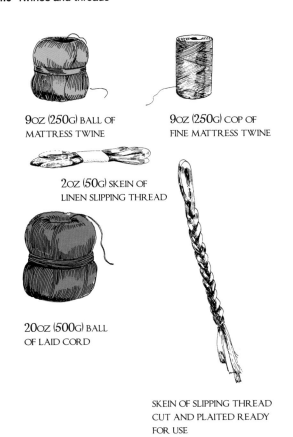

9OZ (250G) BALL OF
MATTRESS TWINE

9OZ (250G) COP OF
FINE MATTRESS TWINE

2OZ (50G) SKEIN OF
LINEN SLIPPING THREAD

20OZ (500G) BALL
OF LAID CORD

SKEIN OF SLIPPING THREAD
CUT AND PLAITED READY
FOR USE

Best-quality flax twines are widely accepted as strong and durable for upholstery work. Upholstery mattress twines as they are bought may be strengthened and made more durable by the addition of oils and waxes. Many upholsterers who do a lot of stitch work keep a lump of beeswax, through which twine is drawn before use. This will improve the natural strength, help to take out some of the twist and allow a certain amount of grip on other materials. A non-slip twine makes for good tight positive stitching that holds its shape well.

Most knots and stitches in upholstery are used to join and hold materials together. Many, however, are used to create shape and to build and hold a shaped piece of work in place. Making shapes with loose fillings is a form of sculpture, with the knots and stitches holding and supporting the basic medium to give shape and design to the upholstery.

Everyone working in upholstery uses the slipknot, so much so that it would be difficult to cope without it. The slipknot may be single or double, and is adjustable until locked off with a hitch (see 4.7 and 4.8). Use a slipknot when starting off bridling, stuffing ties and stitched edges, and for button tying and tufting. The more a slipknot is pulled, the tighter it becomes. Use a double slipknot for buttoning and particularly when beginning stitched-edge work.

4.7 Upholstery knots

A SINGLE SLIPKNOT

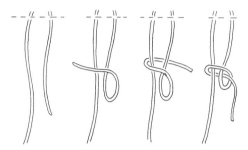

A HITCH AND A DOUBLE HITCH

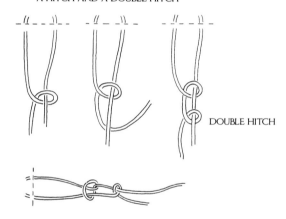

DOUBLE HITCH

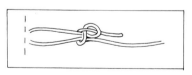

Locking off a slipknot with a hitch knot

A DOUBLE-TIED VARIATION OF THE SLIPKNOT

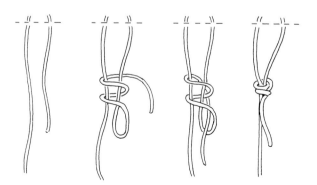

4.8 Further knots

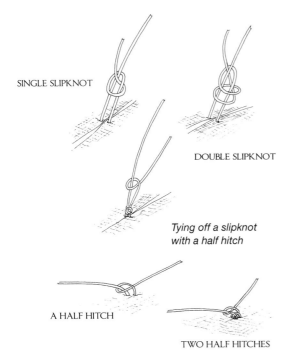

SINGLE SLIPKNOT

DOUBLE SLIPKNOT

Tying off a slipknot with a half hitch

A HALF HITCH

TWO HALF HITCHES

BRIDLING AND TYING IN THE STUFFING

All loose stuffings in upholstery work are tied in with ties of twine (*see* 4.9). The ties are stitched into the hessian with a 5in (12.5cm) curved needle or a springing needle. Where stuffings are applied directly onto timber, then the ties are tacked down and left as raised loops. This occurs, for example, on arm tops and arm pads. Loose fillings such as curled hair, flocks and coir fibre are pushed under the ties in small handfuls to build an even, resilient padding. As the filling thickens, it must be teased out with the fingers to make it even and free from any lumps. Applying fillings to a large area can be tiring work, but creating an even layer is essential. The more the stuffing is worked and teased, the better will be the finished results.

It is good practice to run stuffing ties vertically on chair arms and inside backs: it will lessen the likelihood of fillings slipping down in the future. The bridling of fillings is important, allowing the density of the fillings to be controlled. The more the filling is pushed under the ties, the more dense and compacted the build can be, and the tighter the loops of twine will become.

4.9 Bridle ties

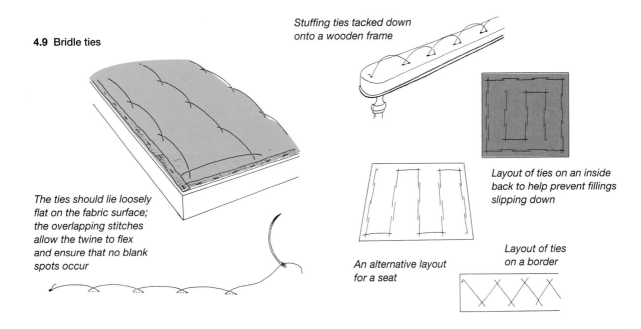

Stuffing ties tacked down onto a wooden frame

The ties should lie loosely flat on the fabric surface; the overlapping stitches allow the twine to flex and ensure that no blank spots occur

An alternative layout for a seat

Layout of ties on an inside back to help prevent fillings slipping down

Layout of ties on a border

FIRST STUFFINGS OR FOUNDATIONS

A first stuffing is the foundation of a piece of upholstery supported by the webbings, springs and so on. It needs to be resilient and fairly coarse in nature, as well as having the ability to be shaped and moulded to conform to the upholstery requirements and the frame design. Good-quality high-density foams are the usual choice for a piece of new modern work, such as 6lb (2.7kg) chipfoams or 40 grade and above in the urethane foam range. Loose traditional fillings such as coir fibre, flax grass and curled hair are all good choices for first stuffings.

Having chosen the most suitable filling, you then need to apply it until it is a good density, depending of course on the type of edge to be built (see 4.10).

4.10 Some examples of first stuffings on seats and backs that have been prepared using suitable first stuffings. They are now ready for the next layers

USING SCRIM

Upholstery scrim is an interesting and extremely useful material; it allows you to shape and form the line of an upholstered edge. Seats, backs and arms of upholstered chairs are covered in scrim after the first stuffing. Scrim is a relatively fine cloth, made from linen or jute, and is an essential item in the building of depth and shape in all types of basic upholstery (see 4.11 and 4.12). It works well and has a natural strength and flexibility. It would be unusual to find scrim used in a modern chair where foams are the predominant filling, but for any traditional work a good scrim provides the first covering over loose fibrous fillings, held in place with ties of twine, while edges are formed on squabs, cushions and fixed-chair work.

Scrim is one of the few materials in upholstery that are turned in and tacked. Most other materials are turned out at their edges or tacked down and trimmed off, leaving a raw cut edge. For best results, use a pure linen scrim or a 9oz (290g) jute scrim. Plenty of small fine tacks – ¼in or ⅜in (6mm or 10mm) – should be used. In many cases tacking should be as close as ½in (13mm). This allows good control of shape and contour and ensures that subsequent stitching is strong.

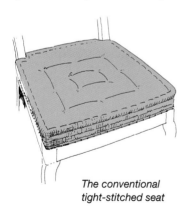

The conventional tight-stitched seat

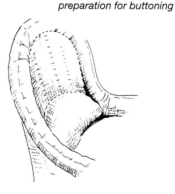

A well base produced in preparation for buttoning

The well seat with scrim first stitched to the hessian base

4.11 Scrim is used to shape and form an upholstered edge

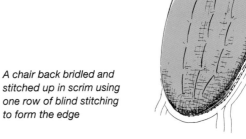

A chair back bridled and stitched up in scrim using one row of blind stitching to form the edge

A hair pad shaped up in scrim, bridled and edge-stitched

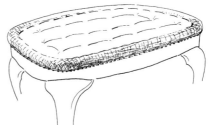

A roll edge can be created using one row of top stitching and careful use of the regulator

4.12 Using 9oz (290g) hessian scrim over first stuffings with ¼in and ⅜in (6mm and 10mm) tacks to make shape on three unsprung items of furniture

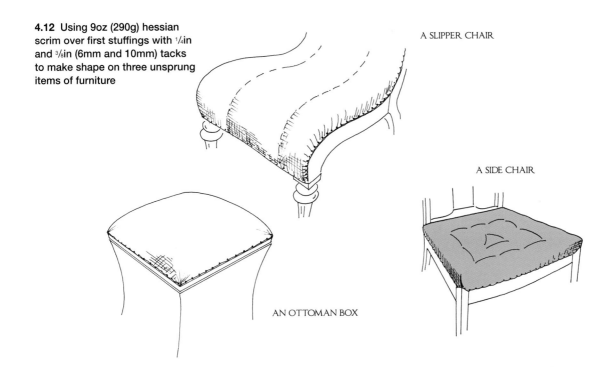

A SLIPPER CHAIR

A SIDE CHAIR

AN OTTOMAN BOX

STUFFING TIES, ARRANGEMENT AND PATTERN

As the name implies, stuffing ties are put in to hold and stabilize stuffings and scrim. Once the stitches are in place, edge building can continue. Temporary tacks or skewers can be safely removed, a few at a time, and the tied scrim will remain square and tightly in place. Stuffing ties are formed with a long running stitch, using a two-point needle, and a medium-size twine. The stitch begins and ends on the top surface of the scrim, starting with a slipknot and finishing with half hitches (see 4.13). The pattern of the ties should always follow the outline of the piece of work; the spacing of the rows is best kept at about 4in (10cm), or closer on very small pieces of work. After the ties have been stitched in and before tying off, they can be tightened down by working along the ties, lightly compressing the fillings. When an even, flat surface has been created, with stitches all at the same depth, then the last ties can be looped back and tied off with two half hitches. Some examples of stuffing tie patterns are shown in 4.14–4.16.

When required, the tightness and depth of stuffing ties can be varied to produce shape, particularly on chair backs and arms. This is a means of creating channels, fluting or pull-ins as a surface design. On unsprung work ties run through the first stuffing to the webbed base, but on sprung areas the stitches stop at the hessian level and should not be taken through the springing, or down to the webbings. If this is done the ties will simply slacken and will then be ineffective when the springs come to be compressed when the furniture is in use.

4.13 The stuffing tie pierces the depth of a first stuffing and holds it firmly in place while other work proceeds

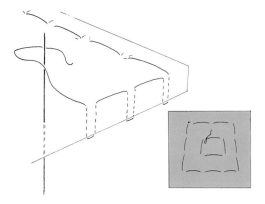

4.14 These stuffing tie arrangements are favoured by French upholsterers

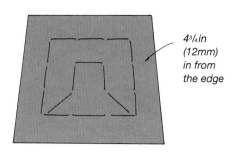

4³/₄in (12mm) in from the edge

A TAPERING SEAT

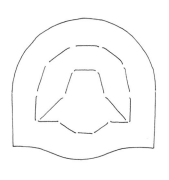

A TUB CHAIR SEAT OR 'D' SEAT

4.15 Stuffing ties

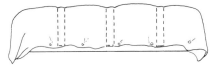

Stuffing ties set into a top-stuffed unsprung seat

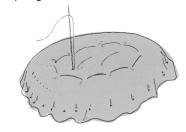

The stuffing tie pattern should follow the outline of the work

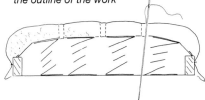

Stuffing ties in a sprung seat

4.16 Stuffing tie patterns

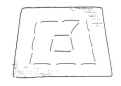

A TYPICAL CHAIR BACK

A TAPERED SEAT

A TAPERED SEAT

Tape of webbing and long nails

Tufts of cloth nailed down

TEMPORARY TACKING AND SKEWERING

Upholsterers' skewers and long-pins are used in the same way as temporary tacks, to set in place and hold materials. There are many occasions when it is necessary to hold linings, scrims and fabrics in place while they are adjusted, checked and matched before permanent fixing. This is good practice and allows for work to be constantly checked before being pulled down permanently. This technique also helps in forming work with a good shape and the aligning of joints, pleats and folds. Use these techniques to set on and adjust fabrics and linings as the upholstery progresses. Tightness, stretch and good line are all essential elements of upholstery, and will help you to produce the sharp, well-manicured finish for which you should aim.

4.17 Some examples of temporary fixings

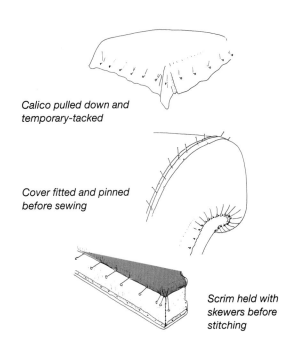

Calico pulled down and temporary-tacked

Cover fitted and pinned before sewing

Scrim held with skewers before stitching

MAKING EDGES AND REGULATING

The regulator has many uses, but its main purpose is the moving and regulating of fillings (*see* 4.18). At least two sizes of reg (as it is often referred to) should be kept, a heavy gauge and a medium size; for very fine regulating through linings and coverings, an old broken smooth point needle or a 4in (10cm) upholstery skewer will do the job well. The regulator is also a very useful holding tool while scrim or linings are being folded or pleated ready for tacking down.

The regulator is essential when edges are being prepared for stitching. The stitched edge in upholstery and bed-making was first developed in the eighteenth century. It began as a roll along the edge of a wooden frame, in which a small amount of loose filling was rolled up in linen cloth or scrim, and tacked neatly around French and English chairs. The roll was held down and made firm by a series of simple stitches. This created an edge height above the timber rail and produced upholstery with a flatter surface. Upholstery coverings could then be pulled over or bordered to give a more angular and sharper appearance. The more rows of stitching added to the edge, the firmer and higher the seat above the rail.

From this technique the well seat developed. It has a high edge all around (often referred to as the 'dead stuffing'), creating a well in the centre. The well was then filled to create a comfortable centre area in, for example, a chair seat or chair back. Often the centre was tufted or buttoned as a decoration, as well as to hold the fillings in place.

As an alternative, a firmer more compact seat was developed from this in which the first stuffing was evenly laid all over a seat, covered in scrim, then stitched around the edges. As the edges were tightly turned in and several rows of stitching applied, the scrim became stretched and taut. This type of upholstery is known today as 'stitched up' upholstery.

Dug roll and thumb roll edging are very simple versions of edge upholstery. Some variations are shown, opposite (*see* 4.19). Fillings for the roll can be coir fibre, curled hair, felts or flocks, or any loose filling that will compress into a firm edge roll. Compressed paper is used in the ready-made version, which can be bought on the roll or by the metre or yard. Sizes range, from small finger size up to 1½in (38mm) diameter.

4.18 Uses of the regulator

Regulating a platform seat prior to commencing the blind stitch

Using the regulator to firm an edge and produce a good shape

Holding a pleat while final tacking is made

4.19 Dug rolls and edge rolls

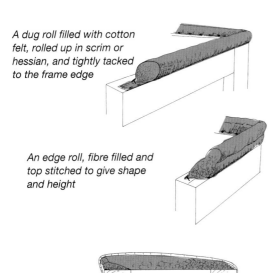

A dug roll filled with cotton felt, rolled up in scrim or hessian, and tightly tacked to the frame edge

An edge roll, fibre filled and top stitched to give shape and height

A loose seat with edge roll built along the front

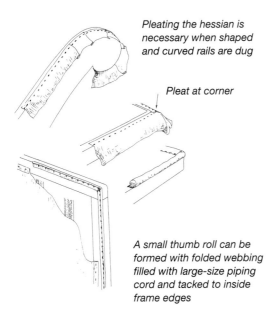

Pleating the hessian is necessary when shaped and curved rails are dug

Pleat at corner

A small thumb roll can be formed with folded webbing filled with large-size piping cord and tacked to inside frame edges

STITCHED-EDGE UPHOLSTERY

The well-seat technique is mostly used only as a foundation for buttoning and to create a soft seat or back rest, or as a platform under a cushion. The firmer two-layer method is preferred for most other work. There are two basic stitches used to form an edge of this type: the blind stitch and the top stitch. The blind stitch is made first and creates a firm foundation for the subsequent rows of top stitching. The blind stitch, so called because it shows only on the face edge of the upholstery and does not pierce the top of the scrim, pulls small amounts of stuffing outwards as the stitch is tightened (*see* 4.20).

Two or more rows of blind stitching can be used, one above the other, when an edge is required to be 1½in (38mm) or more, above the rail. Fine flax stitching twine and a two-point needle are used for this type of work. Stitching can begin once the edge has been made, with good amounts of filling, and the scrim turned in and tacked onto the shamfered rail edge. Make the edge firm, well filled and with a small amount of overhang – ¼in (6mm) is an ideal amount. The stuffing is regulated and the first stitch is put in

4.20 To form the blind stitch roll

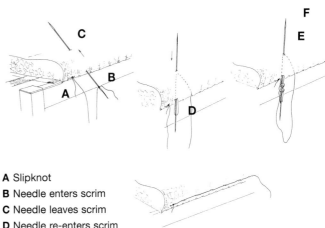

A Slipknot
B Needle enters scrim
C Needle leaves scrim
D Needle re-enters scrim
E Knot is formed
F Stitches are pulled to
   form the top stitch roll

with a slipknot, the blind stitch is then worked along the edge, beginning with a left-hand end and working to the right (*see* 4.21). A left-handed person may prefer to work in the opposite direction. A good firm pull is required after each stitch, and a leather stitching glove can be used to protect the hand from the sharpness of the twine. When a row of blind stitching is complete, the edge can be regulated again to improve its evenness.

Top stitching follows the blind stitching, its function being to pinch and hold the upper part of an edge into a sharp, firm shape (*see* 4.22).

The more rows of top stitching that are applied, usually the sharper the edge becomes. Two rows of top stitching are usual on an average seat edge. A third or fourth row would be used only to gain more height and sharpness.

A top stitch is formed in the same way as a blind stitch, except that the stitches are closer together and the twine pierces through the scrim on the top of the edge and shows as an even dotted line of stitches on the surface. As it is tightened, the stitch pinches the packed scrim into a neat, sharp edge. The size of the roll is determined by the positioning of the needle and the amount of scrim taken in by the needle. Blind stitches and top stitches can be secured with locking stitch (*see* 4.23).

Edge making is an important part of the craft, and once learnt is never forgotten. Variations on the basic edge form can then be practised and used when different upholstery styles are needed. For example, diagonal top stitching is a very useful variation and is used a great deal in Europe.

The feather edge is another development, which simply means adding a final top stitch very close to the sharp edge of the scrim. A feather edge can be made with a blanket-stitch formation or can be a fine, close version of the top stitch (*see* 4.24). Feather edges are recommended when upholstery is to be bordered, and where a piping or a cord is to be sewn along an edge.

4.21 The blind stitch

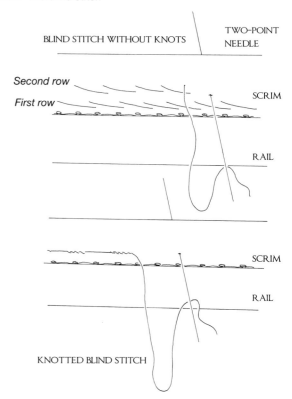

4.22 The top stitch

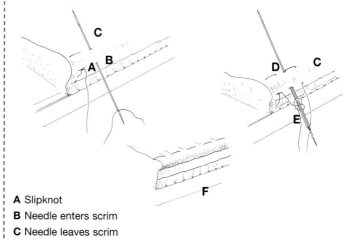

A Slipknot
B Needle enters scrim
C Needle leaves scrim
D Needle re-enters scrim
E Knot is formed
F Stitches are pulled to form the top stitch roll

4.23 Locking stitch may be used to lock a blind stitch or top stitch every six stitches

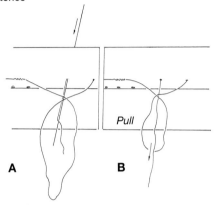

Left twine over the needle, then right twine over

Pull tight to lock, then continue the normal blind stitch

4.24 Feather-edge stitching

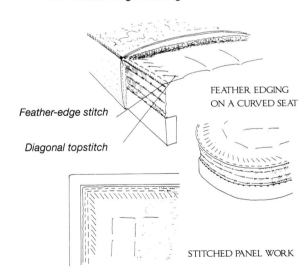

Feather-edge stitch

Diagonal topstitch

FEATHER EDGING ON A CURVED SEAT

STITCHED PANEL WORK

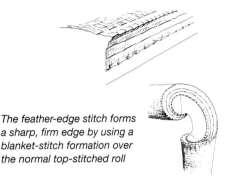

The feather-edge stitch forms a sharp, firm edge by using a blanket-stitch formation over the normal top-stitched roll

SECOND STUFFING, COMFORT AND CROWN

The second layer of filling in both traditional and modern upholstery, which rests on the foundation stuffing or first stuffing, is designed to provide softness and comfort.

A second stuffing can be one single filling or, as in many cases, a combination of two fillings. For example, a soft foam and some polyester fibre, a rubberized hair and some cotton felt, or loose curled hair and some skin wadding. Choose the filling to suit the type of upholstery that you are doing, and make the depth of the filling adequate, so that a crown is created to give shape and comfort. Very few surfaces on upholstered seating are flat when they are first built and covered. This amount of shape and depth will compensate for the initial wear and tear that a piece of upholstery will get during use.

Depth of filling is an important consideration, and the two stuffings can be balanced to give the ideal strength and depth to a piece of work. For example, when a chair back is to be buttoned, the second stuffing into which the buttons will be pulled needs to be of a good depth. This can be compared with the fillings in a plain unbuttoned seat or back where the two stuffings, first and second, would be about equal in depth. Another good example is the lid on a box ottoman, which needs to have a very high crown if shape, design and proportion are well considered and are in keeping with tradition and good practice. Second stuffings are pulled down tightly to set their shape, before the final covering.

PULLING DOWN IN CALICO

Calico is used in dressmaking, curtain making, and as a lining material in upholstery. The upholstery term 'pulled down in calico' refers to a piece of upholstery lined and upholstered over the second stuffing, prior to being top covered (*see* 4.25). It is common practice to line good-quality work with calico. It has many benefits, both to the upholsterer and to the user of the upholstery. A calico lining takes the strain and tension before covering is applied. Cuts and shapes can be checked and made more precise. The final covering of an upholstery fabric will give better and longer service when the upholstery is lined.

The flame-proofing of calico to make it fire retardant has become standard practice on certain weights of cloth. This is always specified and labelled. A flame-resistant grade can be used wherever the type of furniture being upholstered is covered by the requirements of legislation that requires the upholstery to be fire retardant to a certain standard. For example, new furniture produced for sale to the general public or for use in public buildings may well fall into this category. If you are producing or restoring a piece of work for yourself, you can choose whether to use fire-resistant materials. This is particularly so when a piece of work was designed and made before 1950.

4.25 A scroll end pulled down in calico and carefully pleated and tacked

COVERING AND CUTTING

The cutting and fitting of covers and linings on chairs, stools and boxes can be one of the most difficult areas of upholstery. In most instances, if a wrong cut is made, there is usually some way of overcoming the problem without having to replace an expensive piece of fabric. With care and practice, the art of cutting and manipulating fabrics can be learned. It is equally important to learn the reaction of different types of cloth to being cut and stretched. Leather, for example, works and cuts very differently from a piece of cotton tapestry, and the difference has to be appreciated. Some fabrics fray very easily, while some will tear with very little resistance. The range of upholstery coverings is wide, but providing a fabric is recommended for use in upholstery it will be reasonably durable and have good strength.

Most of the cutting required while you are working at the bench is in the shaping and trimming of covers so that they will fit the frame being upholstered (*see* 4.26). Trimming is also required at corners and over edges, where pleats and folds are being made (see 4.27). Cutting positions have to be determined by assessing depth of filling and positioning cover parts so that the cut being made is in the right place and to the correct depth. Most cover parts can be partly cut and partly tucked away before a cut is fully made. This method is safest as well as being most accurate.

By temporarily tacking the piece in place, and using the fingers to tuck the fabric partly away, the depth and position can easily be found. Careful snipping of the covering will allow it to be pushed into place as a test for accuracy. Further snipping may then be necessary to complete good fit.

The method and results of cutting are often closely related to the way in which a piece of cover is first fixed and positioned. Positioning is all-important and must be reasonably good before any attempt to cut is made. Use the thread lines in a fabric as your guide to accurate cutting.

4.26 A selection of typically used
cutting techniques

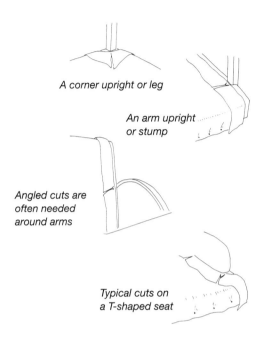

A corner upright or leg

*An arm upright
or stump*

*Angled cuts are
often needed
around arms*

*Typical cuts on
a T-shaped seat*

A The tongue
B The stuffing rail
C The arm front

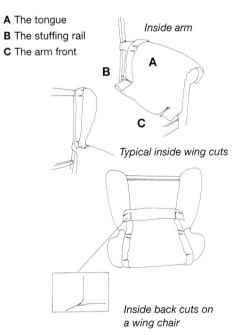

Inside arm

Typical inside wing cuts

*Inside back cuts on
a wing chair*

4.27 Cover cutting at an arm stump

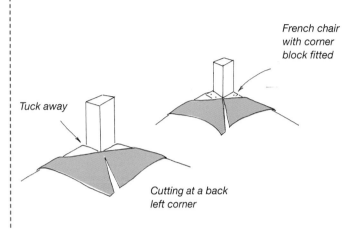

*French chair
with corner
block fitted*

Tuck away

*Cutting at a back
left corner*

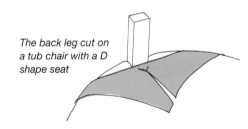

*The back leg cut on
a tub chair with a D
shape seat*

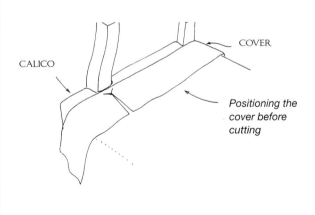

COVER

CALICO

*Positioning the
cover before
cutting*

PLEATING AND FOLDING

It is mostly at the corners of a seat or a chairback that the pleating and folding of fabrics will occur. This is necessary in order to remove surplus fabric and allow the corner to be finished and pulled down tightly and to be neatened.

A well-pulled and tightly formed corner is often the secret of good upholstery which looks clean and well tailored. There are one or two basic rules to follow but as always, you can develop your own ideas and interpret a corner shape to suit the piece and its style. The general rule is for a square corner to have a single fold or pleat and for a rounded corner to have two inverted folds or pleats in a 'V' formation (see 4.28).

Another example is the corner with a long curve or the completely circular seat both of which will require multiple pleating to even out the fullness of the fabric. As long as the pleats are tight and sharp this treatment will be acceptable and pleasing to the eye.

4.28 Trimming and pleating a seat front

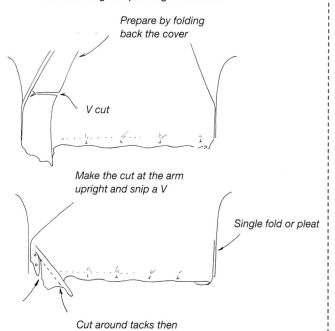

Prepare by folding back the cover

V cut

Make the cut at the arm upright and snip a V

Single fold or pleat

Cut around tacks then trim off excess

ORDER OF WORKING

Each upholstery project that is undertaken has to be dealt with according to its design, shape and function. In chair work the sequence in which the upholstery is built onto the frame is a set process. It applies to most conventionally shaped chairs and sofas. The newer the piece, the more likely there may be a change in the method of working. The average armchair or wing chair should be dealt with by completing the insides first, then the outsides (see 4.29).

1 Upholster and cover the inside of the arms and wings.
2 Put in the inside back and its covering.
3 Build and upholster the seat.
4 Apply trimmings, such as pipings, cords or ruche, to the edges if desired.
5 Line, pad and cover the outside wings, then arms.
6 Line, pad and cover the outside back.
7 With the outsides complete, turn the chair over and fix the bottom edges all around.
8 Add a bottom covering of hessian or black cloth.

4.29 Inside coverings commence with inside arms (1), inside wings (2), followed by inside back (3) and then the seat (4)

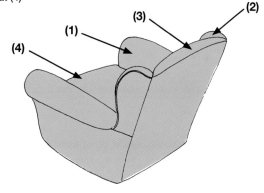

*First fixings at **A**,
then pulled and fixed
at **B**, borders and
facings follow*

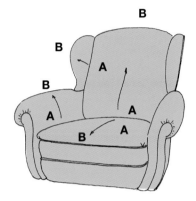

*Trimmings and outside
covers complete the job*

This method of working is practised by most
upholsterers. It allows you to work easily and freely
without being obstructed at tuckaways, and makes
for easier and more accurate cutting.

There is, of course, always the exception. It
may sometimes be necessary to upholster a job
completely in calico using the normal methods and
then to cover the chair in its top cover, repeating
the same basic sequence again. This would be
usual practice when a chair is not being completely
stripped, but just re-covered with a new top stuffing
added to replace the old.

Loose cushions in seats and backs are usually
measured for, cut and made up as soon as the inside
covering is completed. This allows for adjustments to
be made where necessary, before outsides are fixed.
French armchairs are another exception and are
very often dealt with by putting the seat in first, then
continuing with the remainder, as above. This is
because French chairs do not have tacking rails or
stuffing rails, two names for the same thing – that
is, the narrow timber rails set around the inside of
the seat about 3in (75mm) above the main seat rails.

These are common in English chairs, but in French
chair-making steel wires are put in by the upholsterer
in order to create the tuckaway.

HAND SEWING

LOCK STITCH

The lock-stitch seam is made with a circular needle
and some strong linen twine, and is used to sew
hessian, scrim and lining materials together (*see* 4.30).
Making these joins is part of the upholstery process
at the bench. The two pieces to be joined are trimmed
and turned in, then skewered to hold them in place.
Stitches are simply formed by catching each ply,
drawing them together and locking with a single knot
about every ½in (13mm).

4.30 Lock-stitching materials together

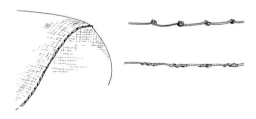

RUNNING STITCH

A running stitch is a simple but effective means of holding materials in place, temporarily or permanently, using straight or curved needles (*see* 4.31). It is formed by running the needle in and out of the plies to be held and fixed. No knotting or locking is used, except to commence and finish the seam. The running stitch is often used as a pre-sewing aid before a piece of work is machine-sewn, and is also used to ruche or gather fabrics, for example, a border or a scroll, or the ends of a bolster cushion.

4.31 A simple running stitch

SLIP STITCH

This is an extremely effective and strong stitch that invisibly joins fabric plies together. It is used a great deal in upholstery for finishing, closing and locating cords, pipings and upholstery fabrics (*see* 4.31). Using a 2½in or 3in (6.3cm or 7.5cm) circular needle (often referred to as a slipping needle) and a waxed linen slipping thread, cover edges are drawn together. The length of the stitch can be varied to suit the situation and the type of fabric being sewn. An average stitch length would be about ¼in (6mm) and would need to be finer for very delicate fabrics. If the stitches are kept small, the join produced can be as neat as a machine-sewn seam. A slip stitch is effectively a closing seam, and so is used where two turned-in edges come together, either butted or overlapped. When a piped join is to be slipped the stitch remains

basically the same, but the needle passes across under the piping cord between each stitch. To perfect the slip stitch, the needle is inserted just a millimetre or so back from its opposite stitch.

4.32 Slip stitching

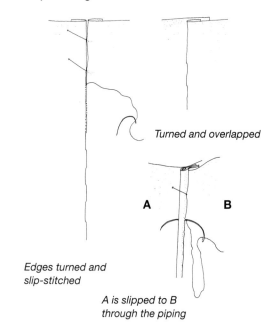

Turned and overlapped

A   **B**

Edges turned and slip-stitched

A is slipped to B through the piping

BLANKET STITCH

The blanket stitch is easily formed with a straight two-point needle or a curved mattress needle. It is basically an edge stitch and often seen in early Victorian stitched-edge work, where a fine feather edge is made around seats and facings. The stitch is spaced at approximately ⅜in (10mm) without knots and is simply pulled into place in order to squeeze the scrim and stuffings to a tight sharp edge (*see* 4.33). This stitch is used a great deal in sailing, where it is known as a marline hitch and is used to maintain sails.

4.33 The blanket stitch

BACK STITCH

One of the strongest hand stitches, which is usually worked from right to left. It can be used as a substitute for machine stitching, as the continuous line of stitches resembles a machine-sewn seam. The back stitch can be used to fix trimmings such as fringes, in which case the stitch would be quite large and would appear on the surface as a very small stitch every ½in (13mm) (*see* 4.34).

4.34 The back stitch

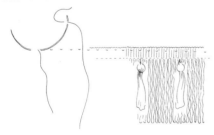

MACHINE SEWING

A seam should be selected for its quality, strength and decorative appeal as a detail (*see* 4.35). As a decorative feature it will depend very much on the fabric being used. There are, for instance, some pile fabrics on which a top-stitched seam will have very little effect, and those are therefore best left plain-sewn. However, the same seam on a piece of leather or plain linen looks extremely attractive.

4.35 Types of seam

PLAIN SEAM

TOP STITCHING

PIPED

FELL SEAM

DOUBLE FELL

FRENCH SEAM

GATHERED SEAM

OVERLOCKED

Piped or welted seams are extremely strong and make attractive joints on any furnishing fabric. Reinforced seams may be used for their strengthening function, or applied simply to enhance an edge or joint.

The plain seam is a good choice for virtually all upholstery sewing. Set the sewing machine stitch length to 10 stitches to the inch for fabrics and 8 stitches to the inch for leather. Only when very thin, fine fabrics are being sewn should there be a need to reduce the stitch length and the needle and thread size. A very large stitch length can occasionally be used when a top stitch is sewn in for decorative reasons, for example in leather work.

Hand springing

Upholstery springs of the traditional type are double cone springs, sometimes referred to as waisted or hourglass. The modern alternatives are tension springs, either close coiled or sinuous, often referred to as zigzag. They are all manufactured from spring steel wires which vary in thickness depending on the hardness required.

Choosing springs

Spring wire thicknesses are measured and specified in swg (standard wire gauge). A table is shown on page 22 of those gauges most used and their particular applications. An example would be 10swg, which is a good choice for the seat of a small armchair. The height of the spring also needs to be chosen, depending on the chair and its rail height above the webbing. Stand a tape measure on the webbing and measure vertically to at least 2in (5cm) above the rail edge. This height will ensure that the springs will work and compress during use without the springs or their lashing being too strained.

The use of nine 6in (15cm) springs is a typical treatment for a seat of average proportions. Another row of three can be added when a similar seat is a little deeper or wider (see 4.36).

4.36 Typical spring arrangements

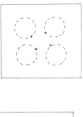

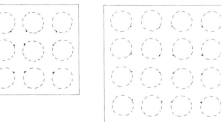

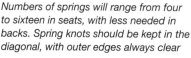
Numbers of springs will range from four to sixteen in seats, with less needed in backs. Spring knots should be kept in the diagonal, with outer edges always clear

Spring layout for a large chair seat

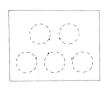

An extra row of three may often be placed over the stretcher rail for the longer seat. Two extra springs are added for a chaise-longue end

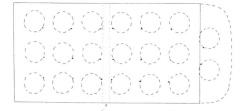

LASHING SPRINGS

Plain lashing is produced with two lines of cord, one running front to back and the second running from side to side. A further two rows of lashing can be added diagonally to form a method often referred to as 'star lashing'. Plain lashing and star lashing are applied over the surface of the springs and link the tops of all the springs in two or three directions.

Another method is centre lashing, which may be used as an addition to the other two or may be used as an alternative. When used as an alternative the centre lashing gives the seat a softer feel, because the top half of the springs is free, and they are held in place at their centres. In a well-lashed seat the outer springs should be slightly tilted towards the edges of the frame, and the centre springs should remain upright (*see* 4.37).

4.37 Types of lashing

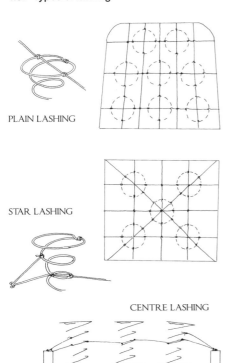

PLAIN LASHING

STAR LASHING

CENTRE LASHING

FINISHING OFF

Both modern and traditional methods of closing and finishing can be used on chairs and settees of any age. However, the slip stitch is still the most versatile and widely used, particularly when small projects are being reupholstered and re-covered. Modern techniques such as back tacking, tack trim, and Y strip, depend much on good timber rails being the right shape and in the right place. Slip stitching of outside arms, outside backs and facings allows the upholsterer to stitch and finish the work wherever it is easiest, and where the cover will turn and hug the frame shape best. Whenever possible the outside areas should be well lined and padded. This is always good practice and helps to give a well-upholstered appearance. Skin wadding, polyester wadding and cotton felts should be used generously before closing and final covering.

The use of bottom and under-seat linings will vary according to the type of work (*see* 4.38). Where frames have become particularly rough it may be best to line and cover up the undersides. Webbed and sprung upholstery, which is upholstered in the traditional way, is finished and lined with hessian or black cotton lining cloth – with hessian being the more traditional – as a dust cover under a seat.

4.38 Fitting bottom linings

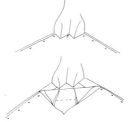

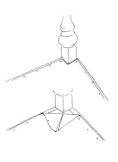

Fitting around a square leg

Trimming around a cabriole

Keeping the bottom open by fitting a lining before webbing

5. UPHOLSTERY STYLES AND DESIGNS

The design of a piece of upholstery and the way it is built are important parts of understanding how a chair works to provide comfort. There are plenty of variations, but most of these are based on traditional, tried-and-tested methods. The upholstery design and its depth, proportion and shape are integral parts of a whole chair or settee. For example, some seats have a loose cushion that provides depth and comfort, whereas others do not need a cushion, but are built using fixed upholstery. Another interesting comparison is the difference between a sprung and an unsprung upholstered seat, with the sprung version generally appearing larger and deeper than the other. This chapter outlines some of the variations and principal upholstery methods from which you can select a suitable treatment. These variations are also very often related to the surface treatment or covering. When a chair back, for example, is to be deep buttoned, then a 'well' needs to be created, so that there will be a good depth of stuffing ready for the buttoning.

These examples illustrate the importance of planning ahead so that as the upholstery is being built the end result can be kept clearly in mind.

LOOSE SEAT OR DROP-IN SEAT

This is a basic hardwood frame which can be easily removed from a chair for upholstery. The frame has shaped and chamfered edges and, once upholstered, is located inside a chair seat or back by sitting it in a rebate or using dowel pegs. Loose seat frames are also screwed in place through corner blocks.

An alternative type of loose seat is the plywood seat frame which is simply a strong plywood shape about ⅜in (10mm) thick, cut to fit onto a chair seat or back after it has been upholstered. Each method uses the materials in a different way. Over time, they have been developed to suit seating styles of different periods.

- Queen Anne (*see* 5.0)
- Regency
- French traditional
- English modern

PIN-STUFFED OR PIN CUSHION

This is a type of fixed upholstery that is shallow and quite delicate. The upholstery materials are fixed into a rebated show-wood frame, and are typical of the Edwardian period. The rebated timber rails provide a narrow shelf onto which all the upholstery is fixed, usually approximately ½in to ¾in (13mm to 20mm) wide. Pin-stuffed work therefore has to be quite precise and carefully built and finished. Braids, gimps and decorative nails are all used to finish and trim the upholstery edges (*see* 5.1 and 5.2).

5.0 Loose seat upholstery in a Queen Anne chair

5.1 A pin-stuffed chair back

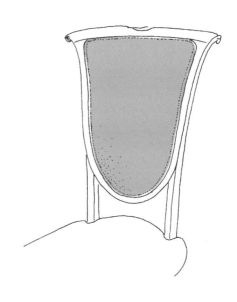

5.2 A pin-stuffed seat

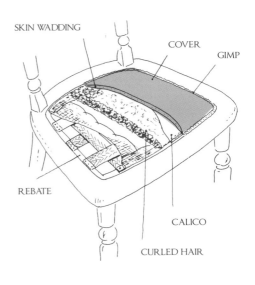

SKIN WADDING

COVER

GIMP

REBATE

CALICO

CURLED HAIR

ROLL EDGE

A roll edge is created by fixing a small amount of stuffing rolled up in some hessian, along the edge of a timber frame. A roll edge can be applied anywhere that a soft edge is preferable to a very hard-edged surface, and where a certain amount of shape is needed to give an edge more prominence and height.

The most common areas in a chair or seat where a roll edge is used are along a seat front, around arm fronts and occasionally along the top outer edges of chair backs and wings. The roll can be made up by hand using a stuffing that will compress well, such as coir fibre or cotton felt. Alternatively, edge roll can be purchased ready-made by the metre or yard length. The ready-made versions are usually manufactured from recycled compressed paper, or may be made from high-density foams. In both cases, the roll must be very tightly fixed along an edge with tacks or staples, and set on the edge with a small overhang, to create a firm edge foundation.

5.3 Simple roll-edge upholstery

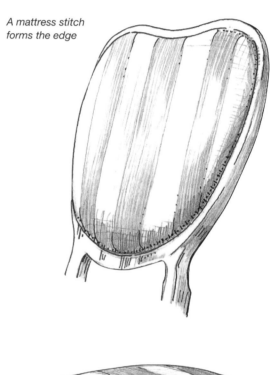

A mattress stitch forms the edge

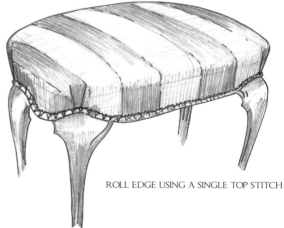

ROLL EDGE USING A SINGLE TOP STITCH

STUFF-OVER UPHOLSTERY

TOP-STUFFED SEATS

This type of upholstery is unsprung and very traditional, and is supported with webbings combined with strong hessian (*see* 5.4). Both are fixed onto the top of the seat-frame rails. Typical of early nineteenth-century upholstery, this type of seat design has been used continuously ever since.

The technique uses three distinct layers or stuffings, and forms the basis for a good deal of the upholsterer's traditional work. The principle of the three stuffing layers, which begins with a very firm base stuffing and finishes with a soft topping, is used throughout the upholstery process, in modern work as well as in the more conventional use of natural materials.

The traditional top-stuffed seat has stitched edges which are firmed using a long needle and a strong linen twine.

5.5 Two examples of stitched-edge upholstery

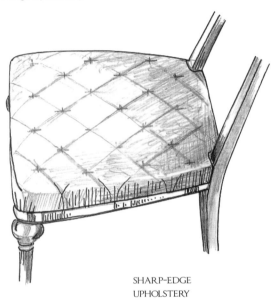

SHARP-EDGE
UPHOLSTERY

5.4 The top-stuffed seat, unsprung

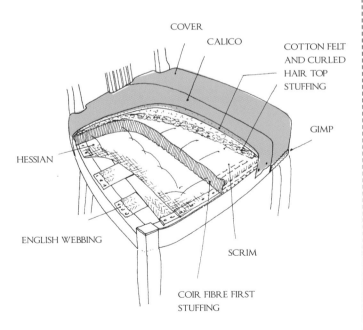

COVER

CALICO

COTTON FELT
AND CURLED
HAIR TOP
STUFFING

GIMP

HESSIAN

ENGLISH WEBBING

SCRIM

COIR FIBRE FIRST
STUFFING

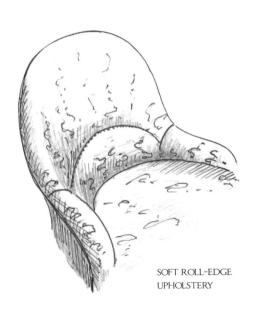

SOFT ROLL-EDGE
UPHOLSTERY

WELL SEATS

The well seat is a development of a very early upholstery method used in the eighteenth century. It has its edges built first, to the shape and height required, which forms a well in the centre of a seat or a chair back. The well or centre area, when filled with the second stuffing, forms a soft comfortable seat of good depth. In many early examples the well was only partly filled, then a stuffed cushion was laid in and was contained by the built-up edges.

The Victorians used and developed this basic principle for their deeply buttoned chair and sofa backs and seats. The stuffed and stitched outer edges in this type of work are often referred to as the 'dead stuffing'.

The tack roll or dug roll seat is another example of a modern development of this same basic idea.

5.6 A well-seated chair

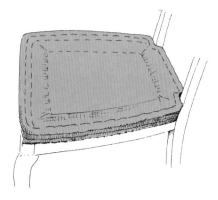

SPRUNG SEATS

A stool is a good first project on which to test your skill and learn the art of upholstery springing. If you use the right techniques and work slowly, there is no need for a great deal of heaving and stretching; however, a certain amount of pulling is inevitable when it is time to lash the springs down and hold them tightly in place.

Sprung backs and seats are webbed at the back or under the timber rails to provide depth for the springing. The sprung seat is very much a mid-nineteenth-century invention, and since then all kinds of variations have been developed. The double cone spring, sitting on rows of webbing, is still the choice for good-quality hand-built work. The size of the spring and the wire gauge chosen will depend on the depth of the seat and the area to be sprung. An average-size stool, for example, would require five or six springs with a wire gauge of 9swg (firm) or 10swg (medium), and a height of 4in or 5in (10cm or 12.5cm). Once the springs are in place and lashed down, the upholstery sequence continues as for a top-stuffed seat or roll-edge seat.

SPRING-EDGE SEATS

This is an interesting variation of the sprung seat, with the addition of a row of springs added to the seat front. A cane or wire is then lashed to the outer edges of the springs to form a flexible platform onto which the upholstery is built. Often referred to as cane-edge seating, this type of work is usually reserved for larger and deeper seating in armchairs and settees.

The Chesterfield settee is a good example of mid-Victorian upholstery when the cane edge was first introduced. These large sofas often had a fully sprung seat, a back rest and arms, all with cane edges. They were the height of upholstered luxury at the time and are still considered so today.

The building of a cane edge is very time-consuming and labour-intensive, but the result can be very grand and very comfortable. Natural cane and wire are used to contain and set the edge shape, and are sometimes found fitted all round the edges of seats and chair backs. The Sutherland chair, which is a large mid-Victorian armchair that has an iron back frame, is another well-known example of cane-edge work.

5.7 Sprung seat upholstery

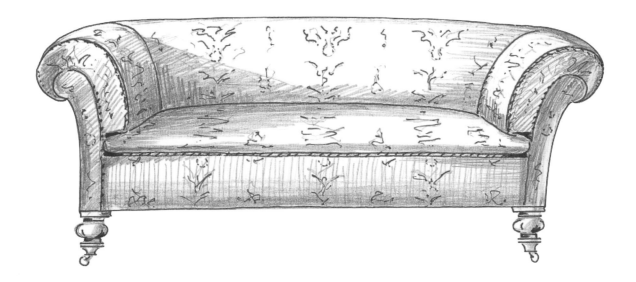

6. UPHOLSTERY PROJECTS

1 Queen Elizabeth II coronation stool

2 Painted French armchair

3 Embroidered and painted French armchair

4 Edwardian dining chair with unsprung seat

5 Double piping and brass nails on Biedermeier side chair

6 George III hoop-back side chair

7 Button border, cord and braid on mid-Victorian nursing chair

8 Pair of Biedermeier side chairs covered in cotton tapestry

9 Beech bent wood desk chair ready for reupholstering

10 Modern footstool trimmed with piping and brass nailing

11 Early Victorian piano stool with reclaimed handmade tapestry on the seat, bordered with cotton suede

Project 1

A MAHOGANY STOOL WITH DROP-IN SEAT

A loose or drop-in seat frame in a stool or dining chair is a very common form of conventional upholstered seating. It makes an excellent small upholstery project for the beginner to try. A seat of this kind can be given the modern or the traditional treatment, depending on your preference and the age of the piece of furniture.

Materials Used

Brown-and-white English webbing
14oz (390g) Jute tarpaulin
Linen mattress twine
Curled hair
New cotton felt
Cotton calico (loomstate)
Cotton skin wadding
½in and ⅜in (13mm and 10mm) fine tacks
Black bottom lining
Cotton/viscose print

Method

1 The stool for this project was chosen for its attractive style that is based on an early eighteenth-century design. The stool frame has been carefully restored. The original beech loose-seat frame has been lost and so a new one was made, and carefully fitted to sit into the rebated edge of the main frame. A space of about ⅛in (3mm) all around the frame edge has been allowed for the eventual thickness of the calico and the upholstery fabric covering.

2 In preparation for the upholstery the sharp inner edges of the seat frame are removed with a rasp.

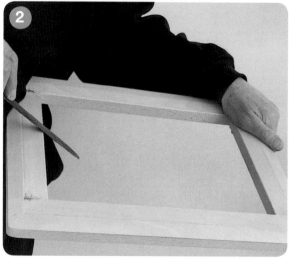

3 Using English brown and white webbing, the seat is webbed with a four-and-two arrangement that is tacked along the centres of the beech rails. To avoid the webbing curling when strained, the ½in (13mm) fine tacks are set close to the web edges.

4 The upholstery continues with a covering of 14oz (390g) tarpaulin, tacked with ⅜in (10mm) fine tacks and pulled hand-tight, before trimming and turning. To get a good tight base with the tarpaulin, the long side is tacked first, then pulled by hand to its opposite side.

5 Now the stuffing ties, which are called bridle ties, are put in to hold and control the first stuffing. The back-stitch formation used here catches about an inch (2.5cm) of the tarpaulin, but not the webbings.

6 Work the hair under the ties, evenly over the seat, to a thickness of about 1½in (4cm). Usually two small handfuls are pushed under each loop to give a good density. The second stuffing is applied directly over the hair filling and is a thick white cotton felt. If this is not available, a wool felt will do the job equally well. Trim the felt with the fingers to feather it off at the edges, leaving enough to cover all the hair filling.

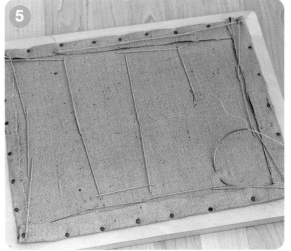

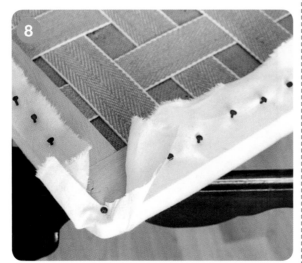

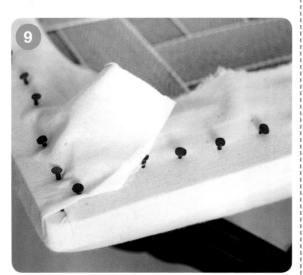

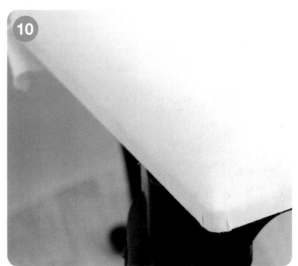

7 Measure for and cut the calico with a good allowance for working and pulling. About 3–4in (7.5cm–10cm) is usually enough. The calico is set on and temporary-tacked, with two tacks at the centre of each side.

8 Work out from each centre fixing towards the corners, adding more tacks as the cloth is stretched over and at the same time along the edges towards the corners. Ensure that no filling creeps over the edge and that the face edge is flat. When all four sides are temporary tacked, the corners can be adjusted, pulled very tightly and one tack driven in permanently at the centre of each corner. Check each side for evenness at the edges and add more temporary tacks as necessary. A small square of the calico is then cut from each corner to reduce the bulk of the folded cloth.

9 Turn in, fold and pleat the excess calico at either side of the corners. The pleats should be tight and as small as possible.

10 When the corners are well pulled and the calico evenly set over the edge, the resulting pleats will be small and equal in length.

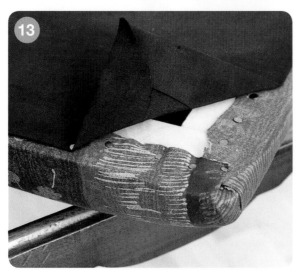

11 This picture shows clearly how flat and clear the edges are of stuffing so that the seat will fit neatly into the stool. A piece of skin wadding is cut and trimmed to fit the seat as the covering fabric is applied.

12 Set the cover on by fixing with temporary tacks at the centres of each long side. The cover is carefully centred and marked with chalk or a notch, which then matches with a centre mark on the seat. This is particularly important when the cover has a pattern. The fabric is well tensioned in all directions and fixed with temporary tacks before the corners are dealt with in the same way as the calico.

13 To reduce bulk at the corners, trim away as much fabric as possible, before folding, pleating and permanently tacking down.

14 The seat is completed with a black cotton lining cloth, turned in and tacked to cover all the earlier fixings. The drop-in seat is pushed well down into the stool's rebated frame.

A SMALL EDWARDIAN COUNTRY-STYLE ARMCHAIR

This upholstery project has a pin-stuffed seat (sometimes referred to as a pin-cushion seat) that is upholstered into rebated seat rails. The upholstery is slim and quite delicate compared with stuff-over examples, and care has to be taken to protect the show-wood surrounds. About half the seat-rail width has been allowed for the upholstery; the remainder is polished and waxed.

Materials Used

Black-and-white English webbing
12oz or 14oz (366g or 390g) hessian
Mattress twine
Curled hair mixture
Cotton skin wadding
Calico
Striped cotton/rayon velour
Oxford gimp
⅜in (10mm) fine tacks

METHOD

1 Our project begins at the rebuilding stage. Many of the large tack holes, left by previous upholstery, have been carefully filled and smoothed over by sanding. A mixture of wood glue and fine sawdust has been used as a filler, and some of the larger holes have been filled by pushing a cocktail stick that has been dipped in glue deeply into each. The sticks are trimmed off level after the glue has set, usually about five hours later. Preparation of this kind is occasionally necessary in order to consolidate tacking surfaces, before any new upholstery is applied. When timber rails become very peppered with tack holes from repeated upholstery work, we have to make decisions about condition, and try to ensure that our intended new work does not add more damage to an already very dry and delicate framework.

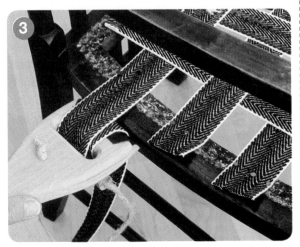

2 The seat frame is webbed with three webs each way, interwoven and tacked using ½in (13mm) fine tacks, along the centre of the rebate space. As a fixing in these conditions ½in (13mm) staples would also be very acceptable.

3 Take care when using the web stretcher directly on polished surfaces. A piece of leather can be fixed permanently to the end of the tool or some form of protective padding used when needed.

4 The addition of a black cotton lining cloth on small chairs, put in before the webbings, is an option that can always be considered. It provides a neat dust cover for the underside of a seat, and can be inserted into any small top-stuffed piece of upholstery.

5 A good 12oz or 14oz (366g or 390g) hessian is tacked and strained, hand tight, over the webbings using ⅜in (10mm) fine tacks. This produces a firm tight surface onto which the filling can be tied.

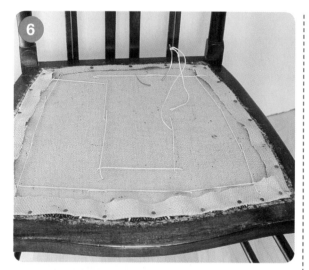

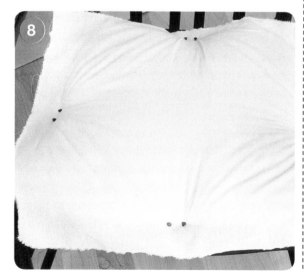

6 Using mattress twine and a 15cm (6in) curved needle, the bridle ties are sewn in, each stitch about the width of the hand in a back-stitch formation.

7 As filling progresses over the seat, tease the hair with the fingers to open it up and blend the hair filling into an even layer, with no lumps or hollow spots.

8 The hair filling has to be well insulated by using a layer of cotton skin wadding, both under and over the calico covering. The calico is set onto the seat, four square, using temporary tacks at all four sides, and pulled to a good tightness.

9 The calico is then stretched out tightly towards the corners and fixed. No filling is allowed to creep under or interfere with the tacking. Beginning at the back of the seat, ease the calico down and add tacks about 1in (2.5cm) apart. Stroke the calico surface towards the front, and fix again. The seat sides are then dealt with in the same way.

10 Finally, stretch the calico hard into each corner rebate and tack down. Check the edges for evenness as the tacks are hammered permanently home. If preferred, all the fixings for the

calico in a seat of this kind can be made with ⅜in (10mm) gimp pins, which are generally finer and have small heads. Another layer of skin wadding is cut and carefully fitted to the outline of the seat, then trimmed a few millimetres short of the tacking line.

11 Using gimp pins, to a matching colour if possible, set the upholstery fabric onto the seat along the back edge. At this point the fabric is centred to ensure that any stripes or patterns are lined up with the centre of the chair seat. A tape measure can be used if necessary. The cover is eased, tightened and fixed using the sequence that was used for the calico. Lift gimp pins where necessary and adjust the tension of the fabric to create an even edge fixing, before hammering them home permanently. Trim the

upholstery fabric close to the tacking line to ensure a finish which is in line and parallel with the chair-seat rail edges.

12 An Oxford gimp was chosen for the seat finish. This was glued down with a clear fabric adhesive, and the gimp was carefully mitred at each corner. The starting point for a braid or gimp finish is usually just inside one of the back corners.

13 The completed seat.

Project 3

POUFFE, AN OCCASIONAL SEAT OR FOOT STOOL

This project illustrates a small seat without an internal structure or frame. It's made from compressed chip foam, which is a waste product from the foam-making industry. It is an ideal piece of furniture for a child's room or a play room, as it is soft and informal. It also useful as an occasional piece of seating.

Materials Used

Reconstituted chip foam (6lb/2.7kg density)
Polyurethane seat foam (35 grade)
Polyester wadding (4oz/110g weight)
Spray adhesive
Upholstery twine
Machine thread (36 corespun)
Black cotton lining
Knitted pile fabric

METHOD

1 The design for this project is a simple circular floor seat made from a polyurethane upholstery foam called chip foam or reconstituted foam. It is the heaviest of the foam grades used for upholstery and is very dense, with good weight and support properties.

2 The foam interior has been cut from a large block and measures 16in in diameter by 10in high (40cm by 25cm). A suitable interior can also be built from sheet chipfoam by cutting a number of circles and gluing them together. The top layer of 1in (2.5cm) is cut from a normal seat-grade foam.

3 The foam is measured from its top outer edge down to the centre of the base, about 16½in (41cm), and this was recorded for use when cutting the covering fabric.

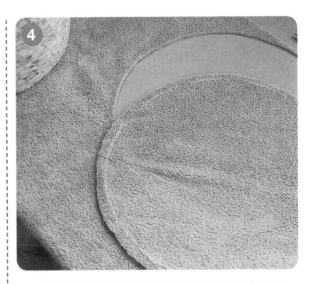

4 The foam is used as a template to mark out the upholstery fabric, and a sewing allowance of ½in (13mm) is added. Thick-pile upholstery fabric, which is fairly robust and can withstand the type of use that pouffes and footstools tend to get, is used for the covering. A soft white chalk is used to mark out the cover parts. If preferred, a paper or card template can be cut and used for the marking out.

5 A fabric width of 59in (130cm) is perfect for a small pouffe of this size, and allows plenty of excess over the length required for the border, or side wall. The measurement taken earlier is used to cut the border height and is drawn on to the fabric across the whole width, then cut. The length of the border is trimmed at the sewing stage.

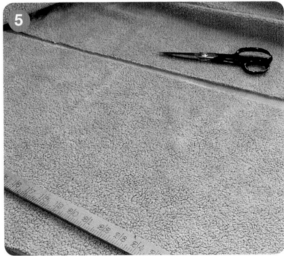

6 A piece of black cotton lining is cut and glued with a spray adhesive onto the base of the foam. This provides a bottom lining and a finish to the base, and hides the foam interior.

7 To cover the foam top and the foam walls, 4oz (110g) of polyester wadding is cut and fitted. The wadding is held in place with a foam spray adhesive, lightly sprayed on both surfaces.

8 With the circular piece of top fabric laid face up on the sewing machine, the border is laid face down and sewn around, using the ½in (13mm) seam allowance. The sewn cover is completed by trimming the border length and joining the ends to fit the circular top.

9 The sewn cover is rolled onto the prepared interior by turning it inside out and working the cover over the edges. By turning the pouffe upside-down onto a table surface, the sides can be adjusted and eased until they are smooth and wrinkle-free, and the sewn seam is sitting well along the upper edge.

10 A length of linen or nylon twine is stitched along the base of the border fabric using a running stitch. This is sewn about 1½in (4cm) in from the cut edge.

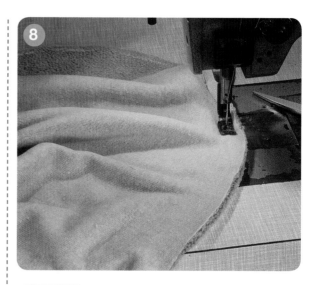

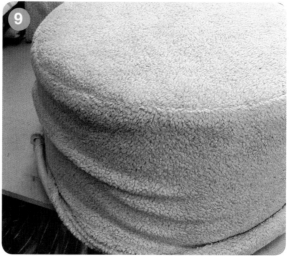

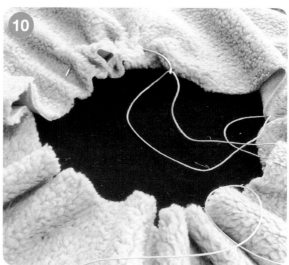

11 The twines can then be pulled tight to gather the whole of the fabric edge into a tightly held circle. The twines can be tied off into a permanent knot, and all the excess twine tucked in, rather than being cut off. This will allow for the cover to be removed and refitted again if necessary.

12 The raw cut edges of the fabric are then turned under.

13 The completed project.

Project 4

A MODERN CHAIR

This project is an interesting chair design, very typical of the 1960s, and is one of a set of four. Except for two main cross rails the chair is constructed entirely from laminated timbers, which are formed and curved under pressure. The seat and back supports are also formed and curved to create comfortable sitting shapes.

Materials Used

Combustion-modified high-resilience foam (40 grade)
Polyester wadding (2oz/56g weight)
Black cotton bottom lining
Spray adhesive
⅜in (10mm) staples
Cream wool/cotton upholstery tweed

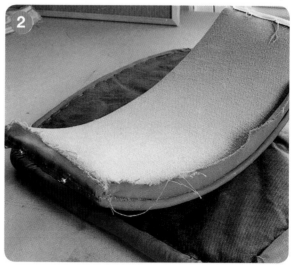

METHOD

1 The triangular-shaped chair frame with the upholstered parts removed.

2 Removal of the covering reveals an earlier original plain mustard-colour wool tweed. A slotted screw system is used to secure the back shape to the keyhole plates in the chair's main frame.

3 A view of the seat underside reveals the four bolting positions. Staple fixings are used throughout the upholstery and taking them all out requires patience and a good deal of time.

4 After sanding and cleaning, the new work begins with a ½in (13mm) layer of 40 grade seat foam. The foam is trimmed to the seat size and glued in place with spray adhesive. The glue is applied in spots to both surfaces rather than all over the seat area. Spot gluing is adequate and is economical.

5 A second layer of foam is cut oversize by 2in (5cm) and glued in place. The four ventilation holes in the seat board allow the upholstery to breathe in use.

6 The foam edges are stapled all around the under edge of the seat ply. At the corners the foams are eased into place and squashed flat by the stapling. This produces a smooth curving corner.

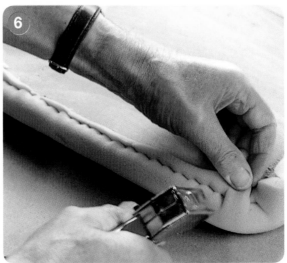

7 With plenty of staples in place, the foams are trimmed off close to the staple line.

8 It is essential that the foams are well glued down across the centre of the seat board, so that they conform to the curving, dished shape of the seat. Working the foams in two separate layers, rather than one thicker layer, produces a well rounded and smooth outline to the seat.

9 Thin layers of polyester fibre are glued over the foams, providing a soft insulator between foam and covering fabric, an essential ingredient in all upholstery foam work.

10 After setting the covering fabric in place with temporary tacks, and stretching it well towards the corners, the staple gun is used to complete the fixing. As always, corners are dealt with last by gathering and pleating. The nose of the gun is used to force the fabric into place as each staple is fired.

11 The upholstery fabric is trimmed as close as possible to the staple line. Next, a piece of black cotton lining is cut and fixed to cover the seat base. At this point the staples can be removed from the gun magazine, and fresh length painted along their surface with a black marker pen. The staples will then match the black lining colour.

12 The back rest is upholstered with just one layer of ½in (13mm) foam and some 2oz (56g) polyester wadding. The inside back and outside back covering is done with one piece of fabric, well tensioned and stapled. Along the bottom edge of the backrest ply the cover is neatly turned in and finished.

13 The upholstery is positioned and bolted into place to complete this classic chair design of the mid-twentieth century.

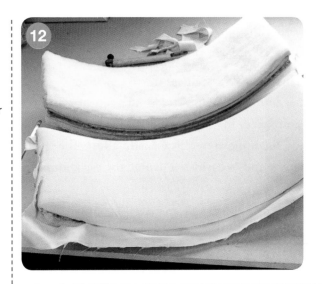

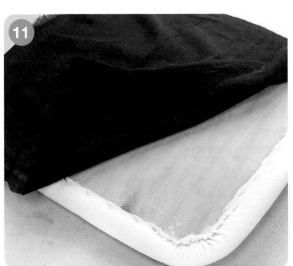

Project 5

A BED HEADBOARD FOR A SINGLE BED

This project introduces the use of sheet materials for upholstery which were developed and first used during the mid-twentieth century. They were the new materials of the time before synthetic upholstery foams became widely available.

The upholstered headboard allows the upholsterer an opportunity to create almost any design shape and to furnish it using fabrics, colours and trimmings.

Materials Used

MDF (medium-density fibreboard)
Rubberized hair sheet
Cotton felt (2½oz/70g weight)
Spray adhesive
Cotton twist piping cord
Machine thread (36 size)
¼in or ⅜in (7mm or 10mm) tacks
⅜in (10mm) staples
Back-tacking strip
Patterned upholstery fabric
Plain upholstery fabric

METHOD

1 The project begins with a cut board of ½in (13mm) thick MDF, to a single-bed width. The height of the board in this case is the same, 36in by 36in (90cm by 90cm). The lower portion of the board is designed to sit behind an average mattress, and so a pencil line is drawn 8in (20cm) up from the bottom edge. This provides a guideline where the upholstery padding will stop. A piece of 1in (2.5cm) thick rubberized hair is cut to the exact size of the board, finishing at the line and glued into place using a foam spray adhesive.

2 A layer of new cotton felt is laid over the hair sheet and trimmed with the fingers to the size of the board. As the tissue paper is removed, the felt will cling to the hair sheet.

3 Next, prepare the covering fabrics and make up several metres of piping, which are to be used to trim and finish the edges of the headboard.

4 10 yards (9m) of piping strip were marked out and bias cut. All the strips are joined together, along the short edges, to make a continuous length. The machine has a piping foot fitted.

5 A 39in (1m) piece of upholstery fabric is the perfect size for this project. The fabric is centred and temporary tacked in place along the pencil line, pulling up and over the board top, followed by the sides.

6 When the fabric is smooth and tight, stapling begins, with the tacks removed as stapling progresses. The staple line at the board base should be continuously checked with the pencil line.

7 A good edge line is produced by tensioning and stapling the corners as soon as possible. Fixing begins at the centre of the corner. A small square of the fabric is then removed so that the bulk of fabric is reduced.

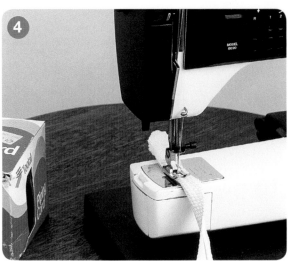

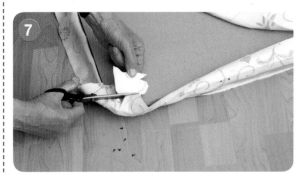

8 Easing and pleating at the corner and some close stapling will produce a clean smooth edge. The outer face edge of the board is kept absolutely clear of the felt filling, as stapling continues.

9 Because the covering has been well tensioned towards all the corners, the edges can be eased gently and the stapling and trimming off completed.

10 Three rows of the plain-coloured piping are stapled along the outer edge of the board, beginning with the inner row first.

11 Two rows of piping are stapled to the outer edge of the board, the third row of piping is fixed along the back edge.

12 The padded area of the headboard is complete.

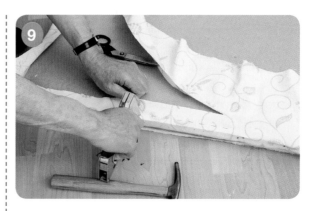

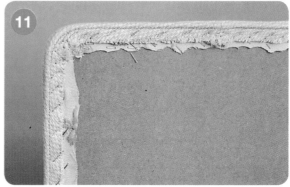

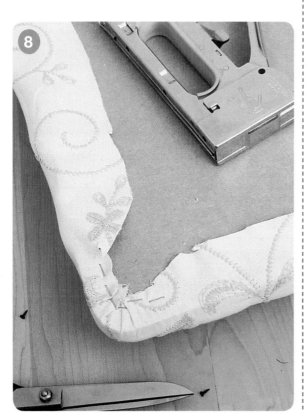

13 A piece of the plain covering is cut to size and tacked face down, over the base staple line, ready for back tacking.

14 Cardboard tacking strip is used to back-tack the plain fabric in place, with the upper edge of the card strip set just above and hiding the earlier staple line. The fabric is pulled down and over the lower edges, temporary tacked and made ready for stapling. No filling is used behind the plain cover panel.

15 The board is laid face down and a piece of calico is carefully stapled to cover over all the previous fixings.

16 Trim out and remove the excess cloth at the corners, turning in before stapling.

17 The completed headboard. A bed headboard can be wall mounted or fixed to a bed base using timber leg supports.

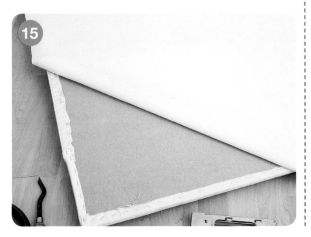

Project 6

PIPED SCATTER CUSHION

The piped or trimmed scatter cushion is very much a feature of today's interiors. Its presence may be functional as well as decorative in the lounge, TV room or bedroom. Our project describes the basic make-up of a square-shaped cushion, which can be adapted to suit your preferred shape. Accuracy in cutting is important; seam allowances should be no more than $\frac{1}{2}$in (13mm) and piping strips $1\frac{1}{2}$in (38mm).

Materials Used

Upholstery/furnishing fabric
Piping cord
Matching machine thread
Cotton cambric
Feather filling
(60% feather, 40% down is ideal)

METHOD

1 To make a scatter cushion of average size, two pieces of fabric are cut 17in (43cm) square, and contrast or self-piping strips 1½in (38mm) wide are cut and joined along the short edges.

2 The piping is made up into a continuous strip using cotton twist piping cord.

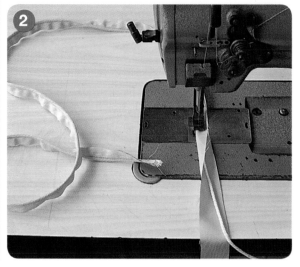

3 By laying all the cut edges together, the piping strip is oversewn around the face edge of one of the fabric squares.

4 The second fabric square is sewn face down over the first piece by oversewing along the same piping seam. A gap of about 8in (20cm) is left along one side for filling.

5 The cushion interior is made up from downproof cotton cambric. Two pieces 17in (43cm) square are sewn together so that when turned the shiny surfaces are inside.

6 About 1lb (450g) of mixed feather filling is needed to ensure that the case is well filled. The opening is turned in and closed by machine-sewing.

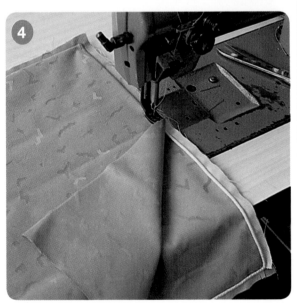

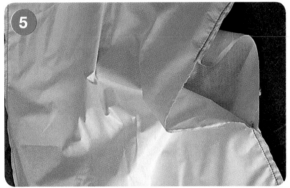

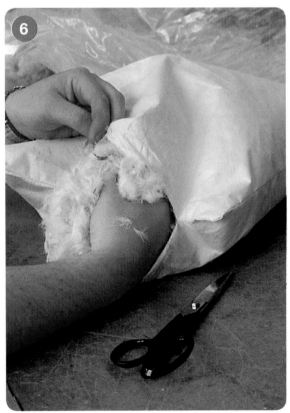

7 After cleaning, the feather interior is squeezed into the cushion cover, and the corners are then pushed into place.

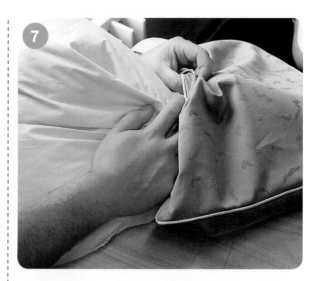

8 A small circular needle and some waxed thread are used to slip-stitch and close the cover along the under edge of the piping.

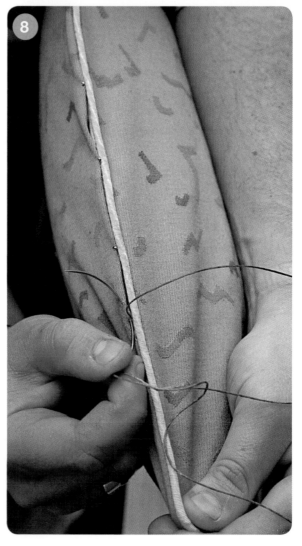

9 The completed cushion.

10 An attractive alternative finish is to make up the cushion with plain seams, then slip-stitch an upholstery cord around the seam edges.

Project 7

EDWARDIAN MUSIC STOOL

Our example is typical of an Edwardian music stool whereby the upholstery is supported on a plywood base and not a webbed foundation. This keeps the storage box free from dust. The upholstery is pin-stuffed into a rebated show-wood frame. The upholstery is trimmed and finished around the rebated edges by gluing on a gimp or braid.

Materials Used

10oz (305g) Jute hessian or taurpaulin
Curled hair
Cotton skin wadding
Cotton calico
Covering fabric
Gimp trimming
Mattress twine (No. 5)
Textile glue
¼in or ⅜in (7mm or 10mm) fine tacks
Coloured gimp pins

METHOD

1 The Edwardian stool is structurally very sound for its age, although the hinges are broken and the brass stay which held up the seat lid is missing.

2 The old upholstery is made up of a small amount of grass fibre at the centre, and a main filling of rag flock.

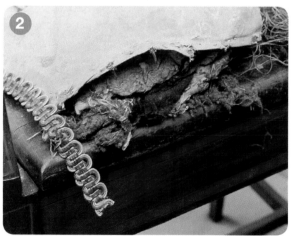

3 A new base cut from ¼in (6mm) ply is chamfered on all its edges, and stained to match the rest of the piece so as to make it less obvious when fitted.

4 A piece of 10oz (305g) hessian is fixed over the plywood lid using ¼in (6mm) fine tacks. A 5in (12.5cm) curved springing needle and a No. 5 upholstery twine are used to fix the bridle ties in place.

5 The stuffing of fine curled hair is pushed under the ties and teased using the fingers, to give an even feel. Edwardian pin-stuffed seats were characterized by their light stuffing, so it is important not to use too much hair because this would detract from the authenticity of the restoration.

6 Next, one thickness of skin wadding is applied over the hair.

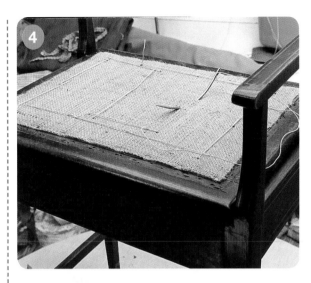

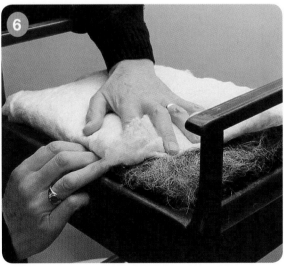

7 The calico is set in place by turning in and temporary-tacking the further long edge using ¼in (6mm) fine tacks spaced about 1in (25mm) apart. The calico is then smoothed and stretched over to the near edge, trimmed and temporary-tacked. The process will then be repeated for the two short edges of the seat, with a good tight pull to the final edge.

8 While the tacks are still temporary, the tension of the cloth is adjusted to ensure a smooth and even surface.

9 The tacks are then hammered down to make them permanent, and a second layer of wadding is cut to size and laid over the calico, ready for the final covering.

10 A bold striped upholstery weave was chosen for the covering, and this is turned in and set on in the same way as the calico.

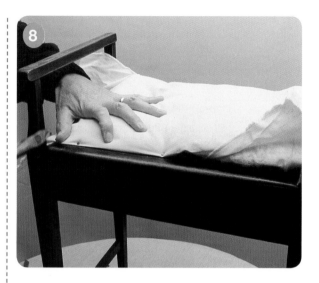

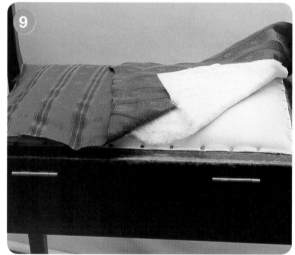

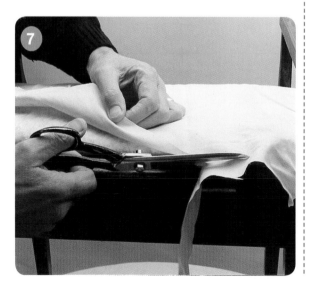

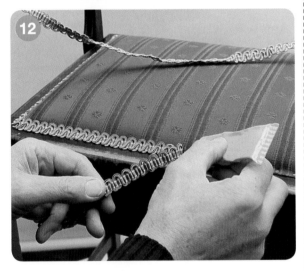

11 A two-colour upholstery gimp is used to finish and decorate the seat, while at the same time masking the tacking line. Fixing the gimp begins by back-tacking with two gimp pins, as shown.

12 The gimp is then glued along the tacking line a little at a time, each section being pressed firmly in place with the fingers.

13 The gimp work is completed by leaving a little of the gimp unglued, which is folded in and pinned down in a neat butt join at the corner.

14 The finished piece.

Project 8

A FOUR-FOLD SCREEN

This project is based on a traditional construction and is upholstered using techniques that were common practice in the eighteenth and nineteenth centuries. In those times the screen was a very useful and practical way of providing a draught-proof and screened-off area. Similarly, a screen was often used across a doorway or behind a row of chairs that faced a fireplace. In today's centrally heated homes the screen is more a decorative feature and will also serve as a space divider.

Materials Used

A softwood frame
Heavy-grade brown lining paper
Cotton skin wadding
Brown-and-white English webbing
½in (13mm) gimp pins
½in (13mm) staples
Covering fabric (this project has patterned chintz and plain sateen)
Upholstery gimp

METHOD

1 A good-quality softwood is used to construct the framework. Each of the four frames is identical in size, and the shaping pieces at the top are cut to a preferred design and screwed in place. This screen is a medium to small size, making it fairly easy to handle. The height is 5½ft (1.7m), and each fold is 14in (35cm) wide. The timber rails are all 1½in by ¾in (40mm by 20mm) thick.

2 Each of the frames is lined with a good-quality strong brown paper. The paper is cut to size and glued with a spray adhesive to all the rails on both sides of the frames. When the adhesive is perfectly dry and the paper well fixed, shrink the paper by painting on water with a brush or sponge. Make sure that only the unsupported areas between the rails are dampened and that the glued areas remain dry.

3 When the frames are perfectly dry and the paper has become drum tight, the upholstery work can begin. Care needs to be taken not to damage the linings, as a half-layer of skin wadding is cut and applied to one side of the frames. This can be held securely with a few small tacks or staples.

4 A glazed cotton chintz was chosen for the face side of the screen. On printed fabrics, labelling is always helpful and should be noted in case ironing or cleaning is required.

5 Three pieces could be cut from the fabric width, and a fourth from another length. The cut pieces were numbered and kept labelled throughout the upholstery work to ensure matching of the design.

6 The four covering fabric pieces are temporary-tacked at the edges of the screen frames and set in position with a little tension. As stapling continues the temporary tacks are removed.

7 A plain putty colour glazed chintz was selected for the reverse side, and this is positioned and stapled with another half-thickness of skin wadding. Each of the corners is neatly folded and stapled. Trim off the excess accurately.

8 When the covering of the frames is complete, the six hinging strips are cut: three lengths of best-quality webbing, and three strips 2in (5cm) wide of both the face fabric and the reverse fabric.

9 The webbing strips are trimmed to reduce the width to 1½in (4cm). The upholstered panels are joined together in pairs, using the face fabric and the webbing, ensuring that the panels are aligned and the patterned chintz faces the front side of the screen.

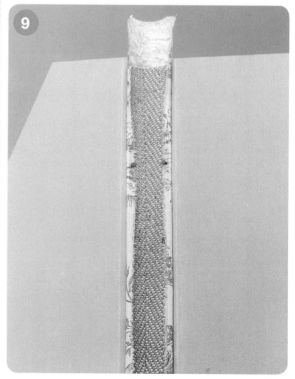

10 When the hinging pieces are set on and temporary-tacked with fine tacks or gimp pins, the ends at the top and bottom are folded back and fixed.

11 With the pair of panels folded together, the tacking is made permanent.

12 Fabric matching and the alignment of the panels should be checked regularly.

13 When both pairs of panels are hinged together, the remaining plain sateen strips can be fitted.

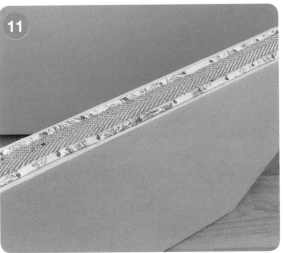

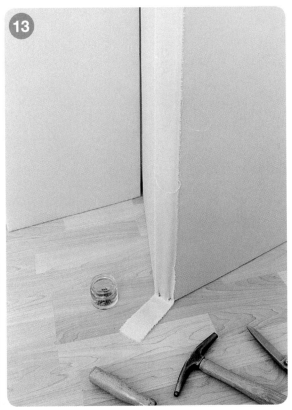

14 Gimp pins of ½in (13mm) make an ideal fixing, spaced about 1¼in to 1½in (3 to 4cm) apart, with fabric turned in and the pins set back from the edges. When brass hinges are preferred, they can be fitted at this stage, before the second covering is fixed.

15 The two completed pairs of panels can then be joined together by hinging the centre edges. Align the screen by standing it on a level floor before carrying out the final hinging and fixing. As an alternative fixing, ½in (13mm) staples were used to complete the final hinge.

16 Begin fixing the gimp or braid at the bottom of the screen, with the ends of the trimming turned in and glued, and also gimp-pinned, to ensure a permanent fixing. About 62ft (19m) of gimp were used to complete the trimming of all the edges.

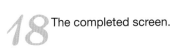

17 The corners are all inspected and, where necessary, extra matching gimp pins added.

18 The completed screen.

A WALNUT WRITING CHAIR, NINETEENTH CENTURY

This project, sometimes called a corner chair, is a mid-Victorian version of an early eighteenth-century design. The seat has been upholstered several times, and the existing covering fabric is a cut wool moquette which can be dated at around 1920–40.

Materials Used

Black-and-white English webbing
14oz (390g) hessian
Curled hair mixture
Linen scrim
Calico
Cotton skin wadding
Mattress twine
½in (13mm) and ⅜in (10mm) tacks
Silk/wool mixture fabric
Scroll gimp
Antique brass upholstery nails

METHOD

1 A well-made chair in solid walnut with a shell carving on the front cabriole leg. The seat upholstery has collapsed and is in desperate need of some restoration. A braid is used to finish the covering and runs all around the seat edge.

2 The design of the frame is attractive and generously proportioned.

3 The chair seat is webbed using English black-and-white webbing and ½in (13mm) improved tacks, in a three by three formation.

4 A good-quality 14oz (390g) hessian is tacked and stretched to produce a firm platform.

5 Tacking commences at the back of the seat, and the hessian is pulled well to the front with tacks set along the centre of the rails. The platform is completed by turning back the edges and tacking a second time.

6 The twine bridle ties to hold the stuffing are put in using an overlapping back stitch. Here the chamfered edge, which is prepared for the scrim tacking, can be seen clearly. A first stuffing of curled hair is put in around the edges, the front two edges are stuffed more densely to create a sloping seat.

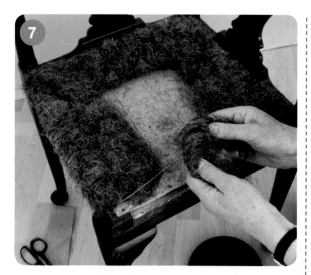

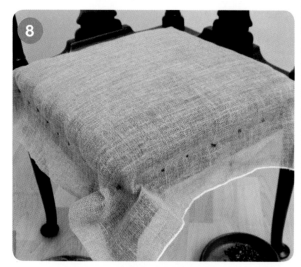

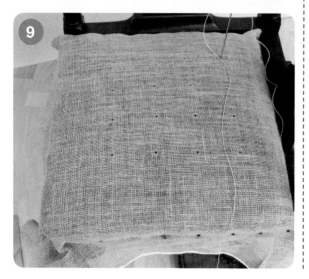

7 Along the front edges of the seat, each handful of hair is given a twist and fold, before being pushed under the ties. This creates a firm nose of hair which is then set under the tie along the very edge of the rail front. This is an ideal build-in preparation for a stitched edge front, and is a useful technique that can be used with animal hair fillings.

8 A linen scrim is cut to size and temporary-tacked over the hair first stuffing, along the two back edges the scrim is turned in.

9 Using a mattress twine and a double-ended bayonette needle, a pattern for the stuffing ties is stabbed into the scrim. Stuffing tie patterns should follow the shape of the seat whenever possible and should be kept well back from the outer edges.

10 The stuffing ties are in the form of a running stitch and go down through the seat to catch the webbings or hessian in the platform. Before tying off, the ties are tightened down to compress the stuffing a little.

11 The noses of edge stuffing are teased out a little to produce an evenly filled edge, and the scrim is rolled under and tacked into the chamfered rail edge. At the front corner the scrim is carefully set around the edge and is folded and pleated, using the fingers and a regulator. The corner should be firm and well filled with hair before tacking down.

12 Excess scrim is trimmed away at the corner before tacking down with ⅜in (10mm) or ¼in (7mm) fine tacks. When the scrim tacking is complete the whole seat edge should be well regulated, to firm the edge a little more and even out the feel of the edges.

13 To produce a stitched edge a row of blind stitches is put in along the front of the seat very close to the tacks. The blind stitch draws the hair filling to the edge and begins to build a firm foundation for the top stitching. Blind stitching needs to be pulled very firmly and a leather glove can be used to

protect the fingers from the fine twine. The knot is formed by winding the twine twice around the needle as it emerges from the scrim. Again, the twine is then pulled very tightly.

14 At intervals of about every sixth stitch, a locking stitch is made to hold the row firmly and stop the previous stitches loosening.

15 When a length of twine runs out, a new length is started with a slipknot; before tightening, the end of the previous twine is wound in twice. After

the slipknot is tightened down, the old twine end can be snipped off.

16 A second row of blind stitching is put in just above the first, producing a good firm edge. After regulating again, the roll at the top of the edge is formed with a row of top stitching.

17 Top stitches should be close and kept as straight as possible; in this case the thread lines of the scrim can be followed, to produce a straight line of stitches.

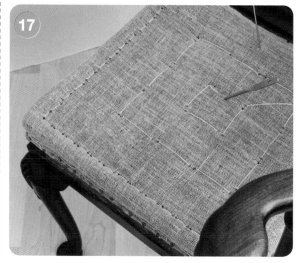

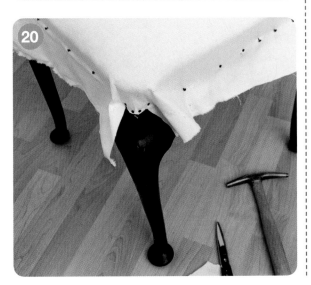

18 To reinforce the front corner, an extra stitch is added in the form of a mitre, pulled tightly using a slipknot and tied off below the edge.

19 Bridle ties are put into the top of the seat and the second stuffing of hair is teased into a thin layer, stopping just short of the stitched edge.

20 The first covering is a calico, pulled tight and temporary-tacked all around the seat. The front corner is dealt with by fixing with four tacks, hammered in permanently, and a square of the calico trimmed away.

21 Two pleats in a V formation form the completed front corner.

22 With great care, using a fine-head hammer, the tacking around the two back edges is made permanent. The right- and left-hand corners are then formed with a single pleat.

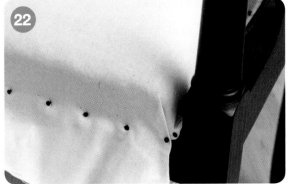

23 When the tacking is completed and made permanent, a full layer of cotton skin wadding is trimmed and laid over the seat.

24 The seat is covered in a plain cloth of silk and wool mixture. The setting on with temporary tacks is dealt with in the same way as the calico. The selvedge of the fabric is along the right-hand edge and the textured surface grain, which is typical of silk fabrics, runs across the seat, side to side.

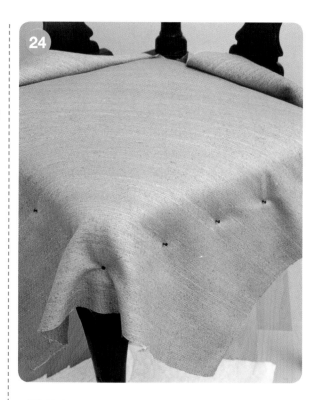

25 After temporary tacking the sides all around the seat, the corner is pulled and set with three tacks. The fabric is then tightened and plenty of tacks added, before the corner is trimmed and pleated in.

26 With the tacking made permanent the seat is ready for trimming and decoration. A matching upholstery gimp is chosen and is glued in place with a clear fabric adhesive. Antique brass nails are spaced at 1¼in (3cm) intervals along the braid, a method often used by French upholsterers for chair decoration. The nail positions are marked on the frame using white chalk.

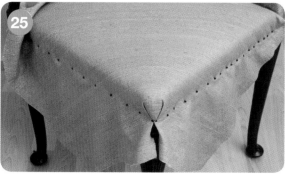

27 As nailing progresses care has to be taken with their positioning, each nail guided in using the fingers and gentle taps with the hammer. Adjustments to line up the row of nails can be made with a nail punch. Nailing around the back of the seat requires care and patience to avoid damaging the show-wood edges.

28 Two brass nails set close together enhance the front corner.

29 The completed chair.

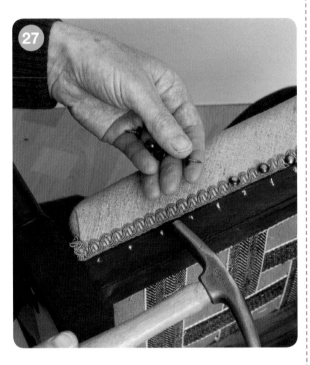

Project 10

A SPRUNG STOOL

This stool with a sprung seat was manufactured about the middle of the twentieth century and has Queen Ann-style cabriole legs made from beech that is stained and polished to a dark colour. The age of the stool can be confirmed by the general appearance and the upholstery materials that were used, which all appear to be original. It was also noticeable that there were no other tack holes in the frame, other than the original fixings.

Materials Used

Black-and-white English webbing
Double cone springs (10swg)
14oz (390g) tarpaulin
Coir fibre (ginger)
Curled hair mixture (grey)
9oz (250g) jute scrim
Calico
Cotton skin wadding
Waxed slipping thread
Mattress twines (No. 3 and No. 5)
Black cotton lining
Cotton/silk upholstery weave
Cotton velvet
Flanged cord
Gimp pins
½in (13mm) staples
½in (13mm) and ⅜in (10mm) tacks

METHOD

1 A thin thumb roll or dug roll formed the original edging with a stuffing of Algerian grass fibre.

2 A handmade seat tapestry has adorned the stool since it was made and certainly shows its age.

3 The frame has corner blocks fitted, which act as a brace, and the rails have a good thickness of timber.

4 The stool is webbed with black-and-white English webbing on the underside, in a four-and-three pattern, interwoven. The webbings were fixed with ½in (13mm) staples. Tacks have been used throughout the rest of the project. The use of long staples is well suited to the fixing of webbing in a frame of some age. The five springs are the double cone type and are 4in (10cm) high with a wire gauge of 10swg. If the seat were intended for constant heavy use, a 9swg spring would be a better choice, producing a firmer seat. All the upper knots on the springs are positioned facing an opposite diagonal corner to give a balanced unit.

5 Using a curved springing needle and No. 5 twine the springs are sewn into the webs, with three knots to each.

6 The springs are lashed with a laid cord and the lashing fixed by two ⅝in (16mm) improved tacks. The sequence for lashing is three rows back to front, followed by two rows side to side, and finally a diagonal row from leg to leg.

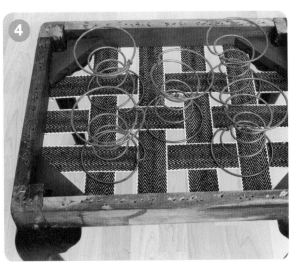

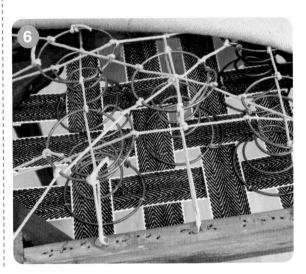

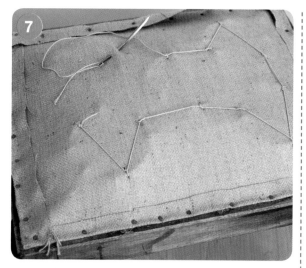

7 The springs are covered with a good 14oz (390g) tarpaulin, and the needle and twine used again to tie the tops of the springs at three points to each. A No. 5 linen mattress twine is used to tie springs to webbings and to hessians and tarpaulins.

8 Bridle ties are back-stitched around the edge of the seat and three rows across the seat in preparation for the first stuffing. The stuffing is a ginger coconut fibre, which has been curled and processed for upholstery.

9 Measurements are taken for the scrim covering from the bottom of the seat rails.

10 A thread is pulled out from the centre of the scrim to provide a centre line and help to keep it straight when tacked on. Using a regulator, the stuffing tie positions are stabbed into the scrim. These are kept well in from the edges by about 5in (12.5cm).

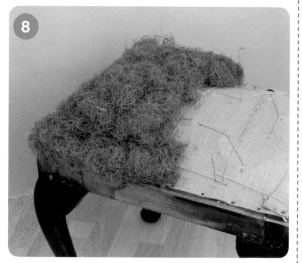

11 Putting the stuffing ties in begins with a slip knot. All the ties are in the form of a running stitch and are caught inside the stool by the tarpaulin. The stitches do not go down to the webbing or the springs. The ties are tightened to compress the filling a little, then tied off at the seat centre.

12 Beginning at any of the four edges, the scrim is trimmed off below the tack line and the temporary tacks removed.

13 The scrim is rolled back and some more filling added to firm the edge.

14 The edges are worked one at a time, filled with extra stuffing and the scrim rolled under and tacked to the edge chamfer. The edge should feel very full and remain square and upright. The regulator is now used to help firm the edge and work more stuffing into it.

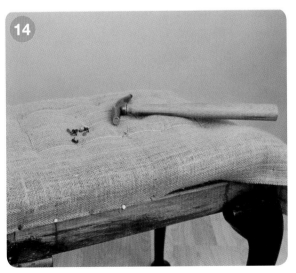

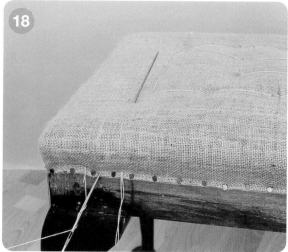

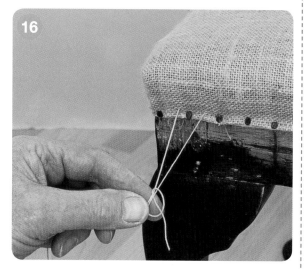

15 Making the edges begins with a fine mattress twine and a double-ended needle, pushed from the tack line at about 45 degrees and up through the scrim. As the eye of the needle appears, the needle is swung to the right and pushed down to emerge from the scrim, about 1½in (3.8cm) to the left of the first entry.

16 A slipknot is then made and the twine pulled hard, both away from the stool and along the stool edge. As the slipknot is tightened the stuffing caught by the twine will be moved into the edge. This technique has been used for some two centuries in upholstery and bedding making.

17 The stitching continues in the same way, entering the scrim at an angle, and returning as the eye of the needle appears. The needle is moved back down to the left of the first entry, taking in some of the filling.

18 With the needle halfway out of the scrim, a knot is formed by two turns around the needle anticlockwise. The needle is withdrawn and the twine given a very hard pull, again away from and along the stool. Regulating the edge continuously as stitching progresses is essential.

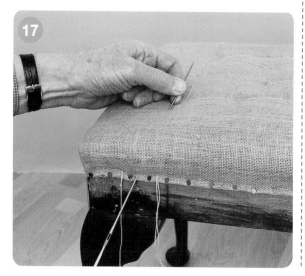

19 Every six stitches or so a locking stitch can be made; take the left twine over the needle, then the right twine over the needle, withdraw the needle and pull tight.

20 The edge of the seat is made with one blind row of stitching and two top rows. The first top row forms a roll about 1in (2.5cm) thick. When the twine runs out, it is linked into the slipknot of the new twine, pulled tight and trimmed off.

21 The second row of top stitches cuts the first roll roughly in half to create a sharp edge.

22 The roll is pinched with the fingers as the twine is pulled. This helps to form the edge and reduces the strain on the twine.

23 The second stuffing of hair gives the stool a dome shape and adds some softness. Nylon-headed skewers are used to set the calico onto the edge, and the hair is tucked inside the roll edge.

24 The skewers are set at an angle to the edge so that the calico can be held very tight. The calico edges are trimmed, leaving enough to turn in.

25 As the calico is turned in and repinned it is stretched tight again.

26 The calico is slip-stitched to the outer edge of the scrim roll.

27 Two layers of skin wadding are trimmed to fit the top of the stool exactly. At the same time the covering fabric is measured a little oversize and cut.

28 The fabric is treated exactly as for the calico, turned in and pinned to the outer edge.

29 Plenty of skewers are needed to hold the fabric, in preparation for slip stitching with a matching dark colour slipping thread.

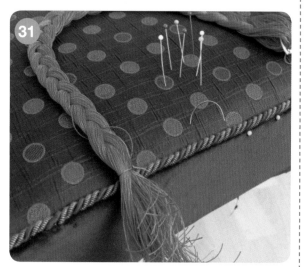

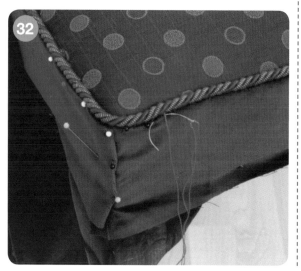

30 A thread is pulled out from the centre of the scrim to provide a centre line and help to keep it straight when tacked on. Using a regulator the stuffing tie positions are stabbed into the scrim. These are kept well in from the edges by about 5in (12.5cm).

31 A cotton velvet was cut for the border. Two widths of the velvet 6in (15cm) wide are turned in and pinned to the flanged cord. A few temporary tacks are used to hold the border along the stool under-edge. A matching red waxed slipping thread is chosen for the sewing work. The border is slip-stitched to the fabric top by passing the needle through and under the cord after each stitch.

32 Each stitch is pulled tight as the cord is neatly trapped. Two of the corners have joins, which are dealt with after the border is filled.

33 When the stitching is completed the border is filled with two layers of skin wadding, folded to make four thicknesses.

34 The border fabric is eased smoothly down and temporary-tacked, and the cuts made at each leg, to allow for turning the velvet along the edges of the legs. Matching gimp pins hold the border in place at the leg corners, and the border corners are turned in and slip-stitched to complete the covering.

35 A black cotton lining cloth is tacked to the underside as a dust cover; this is advisable when a seat is sprung.

36 The completed stool.

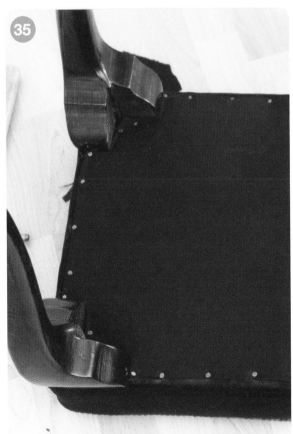

Project 11

A BALLOON-BACK DINING CHAIR (c. 1870)

The nineteenth century saw the development of many new styles, of which the balloon back was a very dominant one. Great numbers of variations appeared between 1840 and 1880 with cabriole legs and turned legs. It was a style that persisted over several decades. Our project is one of a set of six and is made from walnut. Its condition is reasonably good considering its age.

Materials Used

Brown-and-white English webbing, 2in (5cm) wide
14oz (390g) hessian
Curled hair (80/20 pig and cow)
Coir fibre (ginger)
9oz (250g) jute scrim
Cotton calico
Jacquard sateen fabric
Braid trimming
Skin wadding (32oz/900g quality)
Mattress twines (No. 3 and No. 5)
Embroidery thread
Poly/cotton machine thread 36
Clear fabric adhesive
Black cotton lining
½in (13mm), ⅜in (10mm) and
¼in (7mm) gimp pins

METHOD

1 Six yards (5m) of damask 55in (140cm) wide with a large repeated pattern and about 5 yards (14m) of braid were used on this set of chairs.

2 The English brown-and-white webbings were fixed with ½in (13mm) improved tacks in a four-and-three pattern, interwoven.

3 A good-quality 14oz (390g) hessian was stretched hand-tight over the webbings to complete the seat support.

4 At the leg corners the hessian is cut from its corner to the corner of the leg. This allows the cloth to sit well for tacking.

5 Bridle ties are put in around the inner edge of the seat and across the centre, with a curved stitching needle.

6 A good layer of ginger fibre is tied in to a thickness of 2in (5cm). The edges are filled first with three small handfuls pushed into each tie. Coir fibre makes a good first stuffing and produces a firm seat, ideal for dining-chair upholstery. Time taken to fill the edges well to a good density saves having to add more later.

7 When the seat stuffing is complete, a 9oz (250g) jute scrim is measured for and cut. Measurements are taken from the bottom edge of each side of the seat.

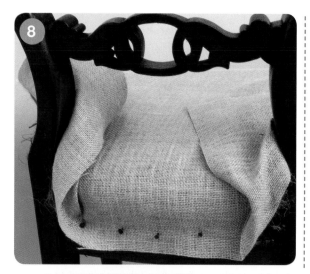

8 Temporary tacking with ⅜in (10mm) fine tacks begins at the back of the chair seat.

9 The thread lines are kept straight and square as the scrim is temporary-tacked all around. The scrim is folded back at each leg, and the cuts are made up to within ¼in (6mm) of the leg. This allows some tuck away for the scrim.

10 Trim away the excess scrim, leaving enough to turn in around each leg.

11 Work begins on the edges, with more filling to be added for firmness.

12 Squeeze the edge to test the firmness and roll in the scrim under the stuffing. On a chair seat of this shape, where there are no straight edges, the upholstery has to be continually checked for shape to ensure that it follows the frame curves. The thread lines on the scrim will drift downwards towards the corners.

13 Here the scrim threads drop towards the back leg. Tack permanently into the chamfer when the edge stuffing is firm. A good overhang is essential if the edge is to follow the frame line. The corners are built by temporary-tacking at the centre and pushing the stuffing in to a firm point.

14 The scrim is trimmed, leaving enough to turn in and make the corner. With two very small pleats set at the corner, the tacking is completed. The edges are well regulated to bring the stuffing out and over the tack line. Plenty of tacks are added before stitching begins.

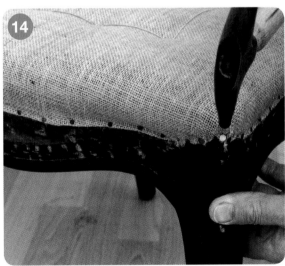

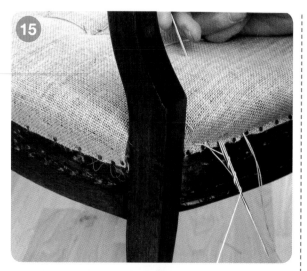

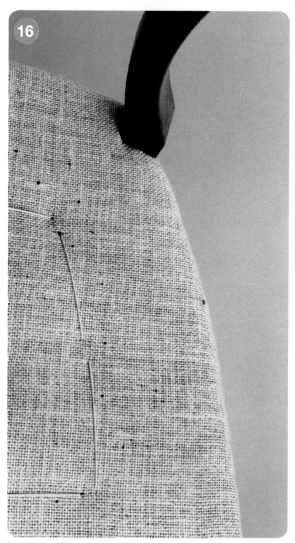

15 The blind stitch begins at the left-hand back corner of the seat. A slipknot is made using the double-ended needle. The blind stitch progresses as the twine is wound twice around the needle to form the knot. The row of blind stitches is kept very close to the tack line.

16 Turn the chair on its side, to check the edge line produced by the blind stitching.

17 A row of top stitching forms the edge roll around the seat.

18 The bridle ties for the second stuffing begin at the back of the seat. The more scrim that is taken in by the needle, the more the ties will flex and tighten when the stuffing is inserted. Ties should run around the outer edge and across the centre and be approximately the width of the hand in length.

19 The second stuffing of curled hair is tied in with a slight centre crown and stopped just inside the stitched edge. No hair stuffing should be allowed to creep over the outer edges. The comfort of the seat is built into the second stuffing. Victorian chairs tend to be given a more rounded outline than those designs made in the preceding periods at the end of the eighteenth century and the beginning of the nineteenth century.

20 A piece of calico is cut a little oversize in preparation for the first covering. Calico is used to produce shape and outline, and is a cloth that will withstand a good amount of tensioning.

21 The first fixing is at the back of the seat with ⅜in (10mm) fine tacks, followed by firm pulling to the seat front. The stitched edge should then begin to show as a sharp outline below the calico. The calico is then well tensioned over the seat sides. Two tacks placed close together will hold the calico and avoid the possibility of tearing.

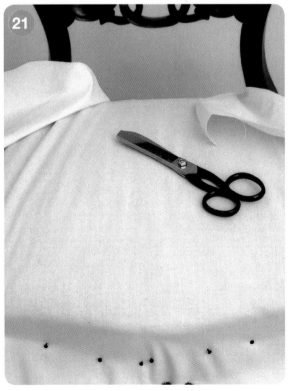

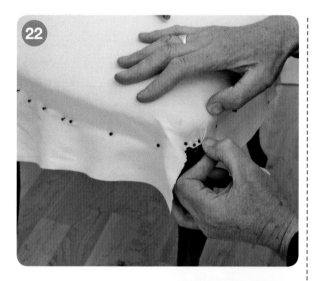

22 Plenty of temporary tacks are added all around the seat sides, about halfway down the rails. The front corners can then be dealt with, and set with three tacks before trimming. Two small tight pleats in a V pattern are put in above the front legs.

23 Excess calico is trimmed at the back leg corners, and the regulator is used to tuck away the cut edges.

24 On a curving seat, a strong pull is needed to clean out and stretch the calico smoothly. The pull is diagonal and down at the same time.

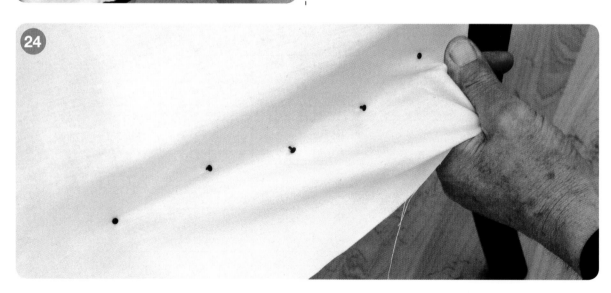

25 Skin wadding is split to produce a large piece for the seat, and at least two layers should be used. The wadding is trimmed to fit well over the edge and cover the tacking line.

26 The upholstery fabric is carefully measured and cut with a central motif for each seat. Two pieces could be cut from the 55in (140cm) width with some wastage for the pattern matching, so that each chair of the set could be identical. The fabric is centred and temporary-tacked in place

using the same sequence as for the calico. Plenty of fine ⅜in (10mm) or ¼in (7mm) tacks are used along the lower edges of the rails, and set close to the show-wood beadings.

27 When the tacks have been made permanent, the cover is trimmed carefully along the show-wood edges.

28 The braid is glued around the seat edges with a clear fabric adhesive. At the leg corners a mitre is formed by folding and gluing the braid and fixing a matching gimp pin into each mitre. The braid is temporarily held in place with pins as the glue sets. The braiding is completed at the back of the chair, and is finally trimmed, turned in and gimp-pinned up to the leg.

29 Five small ¾in (18mm) diameter tufts were made to decorate the seat. These are easily produced using a tufting stick and some embroidery thread blended with some strong red machine thread. The blended yarns are wound over the stick seven winds forward and seven winds back, then tightly tied across the centre with three winds of machine thread. The tufts are removed from the stick and the cross winds tied very tight and knotted.

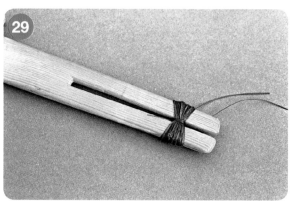

30 The tightness of the cross winds produces a spread of the yarns and a floral shape is formed.

31 A length of mattress twine is used to tie the tufts into the seat.

32 A toggle of calico is used to hold the slipknots and set the tufts to an even depth in the seat. These are then tied off permanently with a double hitch. Research has shown that balloon-back chairs in the early Victorian period were occasionally decorated in this way.

33 A black cotton lining cloth is fitted as a dust cover using ¼in (7mm) fine tacks.

34 The completed chair.

A SET OF LOUIS XVI-STYLE OVAL-BACK SALON CHAIRS

This project uses a variety of techniques for the restoration of the upholstery. Emphasis is placed on the reuse of the original materials as much as possible and their integration into the rebuilding process. It demonstrates some of the possibilities for combining the old and the new, and shows the beginner that it is not always necessary to throw out old and original materials when they are of good quality and can be cleaned and reused.

Materials Used

Brown-and-white English webbing
Jute tarpaulin
10oz (280g) hessian
Washed and carded horse hair
Skin wadding
Calico
Mattress twines (No. 5, No. 3 and No. 2)
½in (13mm) staples
⅜in (10mm) and ¼in (7mm) fine tacks
Slipping thread
Original horsehair pads

METHOD

1 A strong chair frame of nice proportions with the tacking surfaces in good condition.

2 The rewebbing of the seat begins with the centre web first.

3 Using ½in (13mm) staples, a pattern of five and four webs, interwoven, is used.

4 At the leg blocks the tarpaulin is cut to take it round and on to the rails. A V cut is made to the width of the blocks. The tarpaulin is stretched and stapled with ½in (13mm) staples. The use of staples for the foundation work is an option, and was chosen as a less intrusive fixing.

5 A scrim covering put in by a previous upholsterer, is removed by cutting all the stitching.

6 The original scrim is revealed, as well as the original stitchwork, which is now more than a hundred years old.

7 The seat is measured for its new scrim, and a piece 29½in (75cm) square is cut.

8 After a thorough vacuum cleaning, the seat pad is replaced with an additional layer of washed horsehair laid into the seat first.

9 The linen scrim is set in place, beginning at the back of the seat.

10 Using ⅜in (10mm) tacks, the scrim is set tight with temporary tacks. At the back leg blocks the scrim is cut to fit neatly around the legs and temporary-tacked to the blocks.

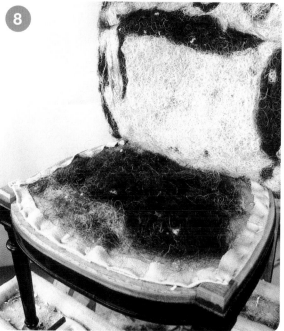

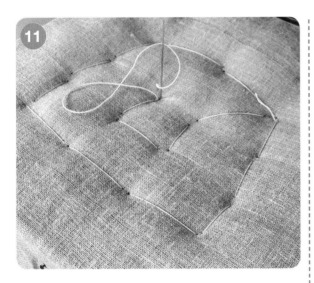

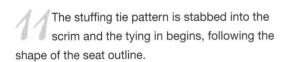

11 The stuffing tie pattern is stabbed into the scrim and the tying in begins, following the shape of the seat outline.

12 The linen scrim is trimmed back, leaving just enough for turning. The seat front is dealt with first.

13 The regulator is used to hold the scrim onto the edge chamfer as tacking begins.

14 When all sides have been temporary-tacked, the corners can be made by tacking the scrim round to the seat front. This tack is made permanent. A vertical cut is then made to take out some excess scrim.

15 A portion of the scrim is cut away, and the corner is turned in and pleated with a single pleat.

16 More excess scrim is cut away from the bottom edge, near to the tack line, and the corner is completed by temporary tacking.

17 Plenty of tacks are added along the chamfer edge, and the tacking on the leg block is made permanent.

18 At the back of the seat the scrim fixing is dealt with, combining the use of the hammer and regulator. As tacking progresses, all the chamfer tacks remain temporary.

19 At each end of the back rail the scrim is turned in and fixed to the leg blocks. The tack stitch, used to secure the seat pad and hold it well out to the edges, is a very old and early type of stitch developed in the eighteenth century by upholders. Using the temporary tacks, the stitch is begun by fixing the twine to the first tack, and hammering the tack in.

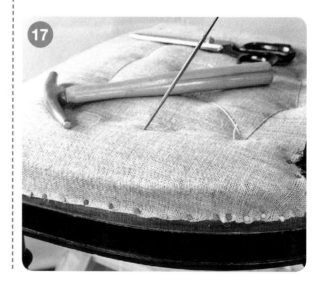

20 The needle enters the scrim alongside the first tack at an angle of about 45 degrees.

21 The needle does a blind stitch and is returned as soon as the eye appears above the seat surface, at an angle to emerge alongside the next but one tack.

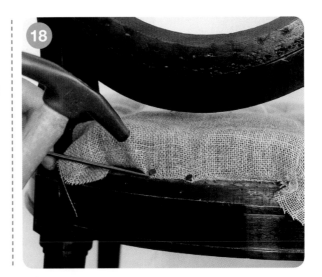

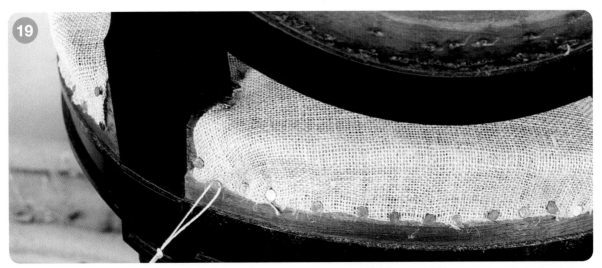

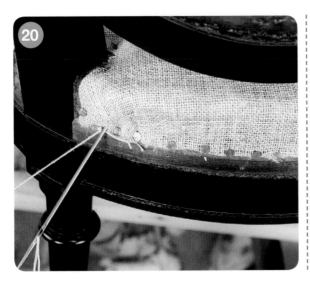

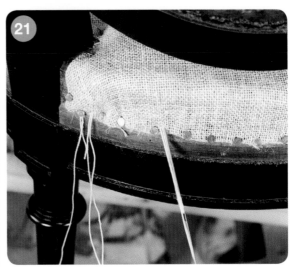

22 The needle is placed somewhere safe and the twine pulled and wound around the tack. The tack can then be hammered home to secure the stitch.

23 The tack stitch progresses as every other tack is used to hold the twine after it is tensioned into the pad.

24 When necessary the pad can be eased to the edge with the regulator, to assist with the positioning. Pulling the twine to move the filling and tighten the edge has to be judged carefully; overpulling should be avoided.

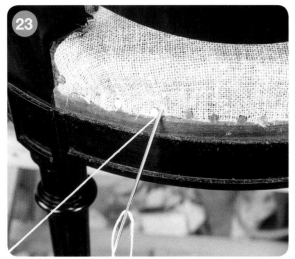

25 When the tack stitching is completed the twines will be almost invisible. A top stitch is now worked around the seat to reinforce and sharpen the edge. This is put in along the same stitch line as the original top stitch, and can be located easily with the fingers.

26 A shaping stitch is put in at the front, above the inside leg point, to pull the stitched edge back in line with the frame on both sides of the chair.

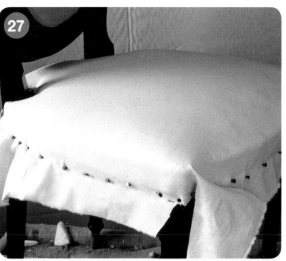

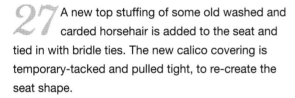

27 A new top stuffing of some old washed and carded horsehair is added to the seat and tied in with bridle ties. The new calico covering is temporary-tacked and pulled tight, to re-create the seat shape.

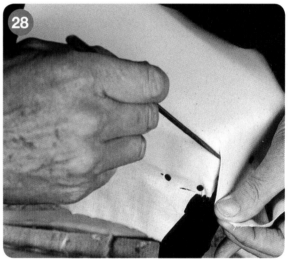

28 The corners are tightly pleated and tacked down, and the calico is turned in and made permanent around the leg blocks.

29 The back upholstery begins with a new foundation of webbing and 14oz (390g) hessian; ⅜in (10mm) staples were used for this purpose.

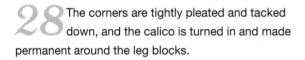

30 The hessian is well tensioned vertically but not horizontally, so that the curve of the back upholstery is maintained.

31 After a thorough vacuum cleaning, the original back pad is fitted in place. This type of upholstery is often referred to as the 'dead stuffing' and is created to form a well for the main stuffing.

32 A piece of new scrim is stitched into the well using a running stitch to attach it to the hessian base.

33 Temporary tacking begins in the rebated edge of the back with fine tacks. In curved upholstery you have to work the cloth in gradually by tacking in between the previous tacks, then again in between, until all the scrim is secured. Some ⅜in (10mm) and some ¼in (7mm) tacks were used. The tack stitch is used to secure the edge, working along the alternate tacks with a curved stitching needle.

34 The holes around the scrim show the progression of the tack stitch and the point at which the needle is returned. Here, two more stitches will bring the needle back to the starting point.

35 The same 6in (15cm) curved stitching needle is used to put in the top stitch, around the edge. A fine mattress twine is used to work the top stitch through the original stitch line.

36 The completed well and top stitching.

37 After thorough cleaning the original horsehair stuffing is laid into the well.

38 A layer of new skin wadding is cut to fit the shape of the edge.

39 The new calico lining is trimmed, turned in and tightly skewered along the stitched edge.

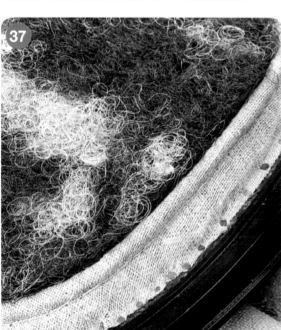

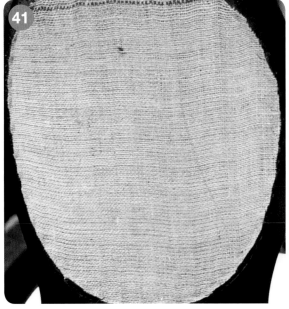

40 The calico is slip-stitched with a 3in (7.5cm) slipping needle and some waxed linen thread.

41 The chair back is lined with a 10oz (280g) hessian, then covered with a layer of skin wadding in preparation for the calico covering.

42 The completed chair.

GLOSSARY

When buying upholstery materials and discussing the work that you are doing with other upholsterers, being familiar with the language of the craft and its technical terms is essential. Many of the terms are historic and have been used over the past 300 years to describe the techniques and materials used by craftsmen, from the early upholders of the seventeenth century to today's traditional upholsterers and upholstery.

ADHESIVE a contact glue used to fix and hold in place fabrics, foams and trimmings. May be applied by tube, gun or spraying.

ALVA MARINA a traditional seaweed stuffing often to be found in chairs made at the end of the nineteenth century and early twentieth century. Mainly used as a first stuffing.

ANTIQUE NAILS decorative nails made from brass or brass on steel with a plain or decorative dome head. Very fashionable in the eighteenth century in Europe and America, and still used today with leather coverings.

BACK STITCH used to produce strong hand sewn seams, giving the appearance of a large machine-sewn seam, with each stitch linked to its neighbour.

BIAS CUT the diagonal line or cut that crosses a fabric at a 45-degree angle. Often used in upholstery in scrim work and in the making of pipings.

BLANKET STITCH a hand sewn stitch along the edge of fabrics such as scrim and hessian. Used as a feather-edge stitch in early Victorian upholstery.

BLIND STITCH a stitch used to create a firm foundation in the building of stitched-edge upholstery. Two or three rows of blind stitching will produce a very firm edge. (USA see SLIP STITCH)

BOLSTER a cylindrical-shaped cushion used as a support on sofas and chaise longues. Bolsters are sometimes decorated with cording and tassels, or may be kept plain with piped seams.

BOXED CUSHION also described as a bordered cushion. A chair back or seat cushion with bordered edges, sewn into a boxed shape with plain or piped seams.

BRADAWL a sharp pointed tool with a wooden handle used to make pilot holes in timber framing.

BROCADE a fabric with a delicate, colourful woven pattern made on a jacquard loom. A traditional upholstery fabric.

BUTTON MOULDS the metal parts of an upholstery button which are fabric-covered to a range of different sizes from ⅜in (10mm) up to 2in (5cm) diameter.

CAMPAIGN CHAIR may be a folding chair or a demountable chair which can be transported easily and easily reassembled, typically mid-nineteenth century.

CAPON a pre-made or tailored fabric covering which can be pulled onto a part of a chair, such as an arm or a wing.

CHAMFER to cut and remove the edge of solid materials such as timber, at 45 degrees. For example, seat rail edges are chamfered in preparation for tacking.

CHIPFOAM often called reconstituted foam or 'recon', made up from foam waste and refoamed to produce a very dense upholstery filling.

CLAW HAMMER a tacking hammer with a face at one end, a claw at the other. Can be used to lift out tacks and nails.

CLOSE NAILING decorative upholstery nails set close along an edge to close and finish the upholstery covering.

COIR a fibre from the coconut husk which is cleaned and curled, and used as a first stuffing, particularly over sprung foundations. May be natural ginger colour or dyed black.

CORD an upholstery trimming made in the form of rope from gimped yarns, and often in various colours, used to decorate or finish an edge. Some cords are flanged to make application easier.

CORDING NEEDLE a small 2in (5cm) or 2⅜in (6cm) curved needle used to close fabrics and sew cord to an edge.

COTTON FELT a relatively modern filling made from cotton linters and felted into sheet form, used as a topping over second stuffings.

CUTS making the cuts in an upholstered chair to allow the fabric to fit around the frame uprights. For example, V cuts and straight cuts.

CUTTING PLAN a sketch or drawn plan of the fabric parts to be cut from a length of upholstery fabric. Sizes can be added, and the total amount of fabric required can be calculated.

DEEP BUTTONING often called diamond buttoning. The upholstery fabric is pulled deeply into the filling with a button and twine to form a design using several buttons arranged in a diamond formation.

DOUBLE CONE SPRINGS often referred to as waisted or hourglass, these springs are used in traditional seating and sewn onto webbings.

DOUBLE-ENDED NEEDLE a two-point needle used to produce stitched edges and stuffing ties, etc. The needle points may be round or bayonette.

DOUBLE PIPING a trimming which is made on the sewing machine using a strip of fabric 2¾in (7cm) wide and two rows of piping cord. May be glued or stapled in place.

DROP ARM an adjustable arm on a settee, typical of a chesterfield or Knole settee.

DROP-IN SEAT a seat or back frame which is upholstered, then fitted into a chair with show-wood surrounds.

ENGLISH WEBBING a traditional upholstery webbing with black and white yarns made with a twill herringbone weave. Also made with undyed yarns which are brown and white.

ESTIMATING calculating quantities and costs so that an estimate can be produced before work begins.

FIBRE upholstery fillings that are vegetable, in the form of grasses or nut fibres.

FINE TACKS tacks with small heads available in all leg lengths. Ideal for temporary tacking and the fixing of scrims, calico and fabrics.

FIRST STUFFING the base stuffing in a chair, which may be fibre or hair, and held in place with bridles and ties.

FLANGED CORD an upholstery cord with a narrow tape sewn along its edge to facilitate fixing.

FLAX TWINE a fine smooth mattress twine in various thicknesses, ideal for all types of stitch work.

FLOCK rag flock and wool flock are traditional fillings made from waste textile fibres. Used today as pre-formed felts and pads.

FLUTING created by stuffing separate channels using upholstery fabric, machine or hand-sewn, usually in chair backs.

FLY PIECE strips of fabric added to the edges of the main parts of a chair cover to extend them at tuckaways and reduce costs.

FOAM upholstery foams are mainly produced from polyurethane. Can be cut or moulded for use as a filling.

FRAME the supporting structure or skeleton of a chair or settee.

FRINGE a decorative trimming used in upholstery since the early seventeenth century.

GATHERED used on chair borders, skirts and valances to produce fullness and effect in a fabric.

G-CRAMP an adjustable cramp in the shape of a 'G' used to hold materials tightly together during assembly.

GIMP PIN available in many colours, these fine tacks have small heads and are used to finish fabrics and trimmings.

GLUE GUN a tool used to heat up and apply hot adhesive, for bonding porous materials.

HAIR horse, pig, cow and goat hair are used as high-quality upholstery fillings in traditional upholstery.

HALF HITCH a knot used regularly in upholstery to tie springs and finish off a line of stitching. Two half hitches will seal and finish a twine end.

HIDE the seasoned and tanned skins of animals such as cow, sheep, goat and pig, used as coverings for upholstered chairs.

IMPROVED TACKS upholstery tacks with large heads used for fixing webbings, hessians and tarpaulins.

INSIDE ARM the inner surface covering running from the seat level up and over the arm of a chair.

INSIDE BACK the surface covering of the back-rest part of a chair.

INTERLINING a soft woven cream-coloured blanket-like fabric used as an inner lining, in curtains, wall coverings and screens, called bump.

JACQUARD a weaving system used to produce patterns in fabrics.

JUTE an Indian vegetable fibre used in the manufacture of webbings, hessians, scrims and tarpaulins.

LASHING the technique of tying and knotting springs with laid cord to hold them in place.

LEATHER a tanned, dyed and finished hide.

LINEN a textile fibre made from raw flax, often blended with cotton.

MAGNETIC HAMMER a tacking hammer with a magnetic face used to pick up tacks.

MALLET a wooden hammer usually made from beech used to tap the ripping chisel when removing tacks.

MOQUETTE a hardwearing upholstery fabric with a pile surface which may be looped or cut.

NOTCH a 'V' cut from the edge of a fabric which is used as a centre mark or to match up during cutting and sewing.

OUTSIDE ARM arm covering on the outside of a chair arm.

OUTSIDE BACK outer surface covering at the chair back.

OUTSIDE WING the outer covering fabric on the wing of a wing armchair.

PASSEMENTERIE the French term used to describe all kinds of trimmings and decoration in furnishing.

PILE FABRIC those woven fabrics with a surface pile, for example, velour, velvet and corduroy.

PINCERS the tool used to lift out nails and tacks from wood surfaces.

PIPING FOOT a sewing machine presser foot with a grooved sole, designed specifically for making piping.

PLATFORM the seat in a chair which is upholstered in preparation for supporting a fitted cushion.

POLYESTER FIBRE a soft white wadding made in several weights and thicknesses. Also produced in loose form as a cushion filling. Used most successfully as a wrap under upholstery fabric.

PULL-IN a channel produced in a chair back by deep stitching, giving shape and form to a surface. It is a French technique.

RAILS the main timber parts of a chair frame.

RASP a tool used to remove the sharp edges on timber frames and produce chamfers prior to tacking down scrim.

REBATE a recess cut into timber rails in order to house fixed or drop-in upholstery.

REGULATOR an upholstery tool made from steel with a sharp point and a flat end; the regulator has many uses, particularly the regulating and moving of stuffings.

RIPPER a ripping chisel used to remove tacks and staples; may be straight-bladed or cranked.

ROLL EDGE a shaped edge in the form of a roll of stuffing held down with scrim or calico, and tacked in place.

ROSETTE a circular trimming created with a fabric, a cord or a gimped yarn, used on its own or with a tassel.

RUBBERIZED HAIR a sheet filling material made from animal hair bonded with natural and synthetic rubbers, usually 1in (25mm) thick.

SCRIM a loosely woven fabric made from linen or jute, used to mould the first stuffing and the stitched edges in good-quality upholstery.

SEAM ALLOWANCE the ⅜in (10mm) or ½in (13mm) margin allowed when two fabrics are being machine sewn.

SECOND STUFFING the soft layer of filling tied in over scrim before the calico covering. Usually curled hair or wool felt.

SELF-PIPING a single piping made up from the upholstery fabric, usually bias cut.

SHOW-WOOD the visible polished or painted surface on a chair frame.

SKEWERS long upholstery pins used to secure materials prior to sewing. The most common lengths used are 3in and 4in (7.5cm and 10cm).

SLIP STITCH a handmade closing seam using waxed linen thread and a curved needle.

SPRING CANVAS a heavyweight hessian 14oz (390g) and above, known as tarpaulin, and used over spring foundations.

SPRING NEEDLE a 5in (12.5cm) curved needle used to tie springs in place onto webbing bases.

SQUAB a slim cushion pad filled with curled hair, wool fleece or feathers, used mainly in seating.

STOCKINETTE a lightweight knitted fabric made from cotton or polyester, and used over foam and fibre interiors.

STUFFING TIES deep ties made with twine to hold a first stuffing in place.

TACK ROLL often called a dug roll. The firm edge made with hessian or scrim and a core filling of hair, fibre or felt.

TACKS the traditional upholstery fixing available in fine and improved qualities and various lengths.

TAILORS' CHALK used for marking out fabrics and linings, and available in several colours.

TAPESTRY a handmade or machine-made fabric of good weight. Traditionally used as a decorative covering for seating.

TEASE the technique used to open up and separate fibre and hair stuffing to produce a fine soft surface.

TEMPORARY TACK tacks which are used to set the position of materials on a chair frame and are hammered only halfway into the timber; can be removed quickly.

TOP STITCH a knotted edge stitch produced with a double-ended needle to create a firm sharp edge line.

TUCKAWAY fabrics and linings pushed out of sight at the point where inside backs and inside arms meet a seat.

TUFTS may be functional or decorative, and in the form of a small floret of wool or silk. Used in upholstery and mattress making to contain and hold stuffed components; an early form of buttoning.

WADDING a fine cotton filling known as skin wadding and used over second stuffings and over calico to hold back other fibrous fillings.

WARP the threads or yarns that run the length of a fabric.

WEFT the threads or yarns that run across the width of a woven fabric.

Metric Conversion Table

Inches	mm	Inches	mm	Inches	mm	Inches	mm	Inches	mm
¼	6	3¼	83	7¼	185	19	485	40	1015
⅜	10	3½	88	7½	190	20	510	41	1040
½	13	3⅝	92	7¾	195	21	535	42	1065
⅝	16	3¾	95	8	200	22	560	43	1090
¾	19	4	100	8¼	210	23	585	44	1120
⅞	22	4⅛	105	8½	215	24	610	45	1145
1	25	4¼–4⅜	110	8¾	220	25	635	46	1170
1⅛	30	4½	115	9	230	26	660	47	1195
1¼	32	4¾	120	9¼	235	27	685	48	1220
1⅜	35	5	125	9½	240	28	710	49	1245
1½	38	5⅛	130	9¾	250	29	735	50	1270
1⅝	40	5¼	133	10	255	30	760	51	1295
1¾	45	5½	140	10⅛	257	31	785	52	1320
2	50	5¾	145	11	280	32	815	53	1345
2⅛–2¼	55	6	150	12	305	33	840	54	1370
2⅜	60	6⅛	155	13	330	34	865	55	1395
2½	63	6¼	160	14	355	35	890	56	1420
2⅝	65	6½	165	15	380	36	915	57	1450
2¾	70	6¾	170	16	405	37	940	58	1475
3	75	7	178	17	430	38	965	59	1500
3⅛	80	7⅛	180	18	460	39	990	60	1525

To obtain the metric size for dimensions under 60in, not shown in the above table, multiply the imperial size in inches by 25.4 and round to the nearest millimetre, taking 0.5mm upwards.

e.g. 9⅛ x 25.4 = 231.8, say 232mm

To obtain the metric size for dimensions over 60in, multiply the imperial size in inches by 25.4 and round to the nearest 10mm, taking 5mm upwards.

e.g. 67 x 25.4 = 1701.8, say 1700mm

USEFUL ADDRESSES

Association of Master
Upholsterers and Soft Furnishers
Francis Vaughan House, Q1
Capital Point Business Centre,
Capital Business Park, Parkway,
Cardiff CF3 2PU, UK
www.upholsterers.co.uk

British Antique Furniture
Restorers' Association (BAFRA)
The Old Rectory, Warmwell,
Dorchester, Dorset DT2 8HQ, UK
www.bafra.org.uk

British Furniture Manufacturers'
Association
Wycombe House, 9 Amersham
Hill, High Wycombe, Bucks
HP13 6NR, UK
www.bfm.org.uk

Buckinghamshire Chilterns
University College
Design Faculty, Queen Alexandra
Road, High Wycombe, Bucks
HP11 2JZ, UK
www.bucks.ac.uk

Chambre d'Apprentissage
Des Industiries de 1'Amb, 200
Bis Boulevard Voltaire
75 011 Paris, France

City and Guilds of London
Institute
1 Giltspur Street, London
EC1A 9DD, UK
www.city-and-guilds.com

The Countryside Agency
John Dower House,
Crescent Place, Cheltenham,
Gloucestershire GL50 3RA, UK
www.countrysideaccess.gov.uk

The Crafts Council
44a Pentonville Road, Islington,
London N1 9BY, UK
www.craftscouncil.org.uk

Department for Business,
Enterprise and Regulatory
Reform
Ministerial Correspondence
Unit, 1 Victoria Street, London
SW1H 0ET
www.berr.gov.uk

Design Council
34 Bow Street, London
WC2E 7DL, UK
www.design-council.org.uk

Furniture, Furnishings and
Interiors National Training
Organisation (FFINTO)
67 Wollaton Road, Beeston,
Nottingham NG9 2NG, UK
www.ffinto.org

Furniture Industry Research
Association
Maxwell Road, Stevenage,
Hertfordshire SG1 2EW, UK
www.fira.co.uk

Geffrye Museum
Kingsland Road, London
E2 8EA, UK
www.geffrye-museum.org.uk

Guild of Traditional Upholsterers
Feather Barn, Cox Park,
Nr Gunnislake, Cornwall
PL18 9BB, UK
www.gtu.org.uk

London Metropolitan University
41-71 Commercial Road,
London E1 1LA, UK
www.londonmet.ac.uk

The National Council for
Vocational Qualifications
83 Piccadilly, London
W1J 8QA, UK
www.qca.org.uk

National Trust
36 Queen Anne's Gate,
London SW1H 9AS, UK
www.nationaltrust.org.uk

Upholstery Manufacturing
Magazine
Published by Watt Publishing,
Illinois USA
www.fdmonline.com

Victoria and Albert Museum
Cromwell Road, South
Kensington, London
SW7 2RL, UK
www.vam.ac.uk

TABLE OF UK/USA UPHOLSTERY TERMS

UK TERMS	USA TERMS
Roll or piece	Bolt of fabric
Loose seat	Slip seat
Cutting plan	Cutting chart
Border	Boxing strip
Fibre	Moss
Hessian	Burlap
Wadding	Batting
Calico	Muslin
Edge Roll	Stuffed roll
Piping cord	Welt cord
Zig-zag	No-sag
Dished seat	Sag seat
Spring unit	Marshall unit
Back spring	Pillow spring
Lashed	Tied
Regulator	Stuffing skewer
Gimp pins	Gimp tacks
Valences	Flounces
Stool	Ottoman
Loose cover	Slip cover
Ruching	Gathering
Tub chair	Barrel chair
Ruche	Loop fringe
Fluting	Channeling
Buttoning	Tufting
Wool felt	Excelsior
Bottoming	Cambric
Ripping chisel	Tack puller
Dug roll	Frame edging
Platform	Seat front
Slip stitching	Blind stitching
Back tacking	Blind tacking
Double-cone springs	Coil springs
Fly	Stretcher
Double piping	Double cording
Close nailing	Nail trim

ABOUT THE AUTHOR

A lecturer for over 40 years on upholstery restoration and craftsmanship, David James is an honorary member of the City and Guilds of London Institute and has been awarded their licentiateship. He is also a member of the Guild of Traditional Upholsterers. He is the renowned author of six previous upholstery titles published by GMC Publications: the standard work on the subject *Upholstery: A Complete Course (Revised Edition)*, *Upholstery Techniques & Projects*, *Upholstery Restoration*, *Upholstery Tips and Hints*, *The Upholsterer's Pocket Reference Book* and *Upholstery A Beginners' Guide*.

INDEX

To request a full catalogue of GMC titles, please contact:

GMC Publications
Castle Place
166 High Street
Lewes
East Sussex
BN7 1XU
United Kingdom

Tel: 01273 488005
Fax: 01273 402866

www.thegmcgroup.com